Living an Extraordinary Life in an Ordinary Reality

Just Show Up, Listen and Demonstrate

Living an Extraordinary Life in an Ordinary Reality

Just Show Up, Listen and Demonstrate

Jim Young

BOOKS

Winchester, UK
Washington, USA

First published by O-Books, 2011
O-Books is an imprint of John Hunt Publishing Ltd., Laurel House, Station Approach,
Alresford, Hants, SO24 9JH, UK
office1@o-books.net
www.o-books.com

For distributor details and how to order please visit the 'Ordering' section on our website.

Text copyright: Jim Young 2010

ISBN: 978 1 84694 703 2

A CIP catalogue record for this book is available from the British Library.

Cover image, Jesus Laughing, by Ralph Kozak.
Copyright, 1977, Praise Screen Prints
2900 W. Armstrong Lake Trail, Empire, MI 49630
Used with permission: jesuslaughing.com

Worldshift Movement (www.worldshiftmovement.org)
Worldshift Media (www.worldshiftmedia.org)

Design: Lee Nash

Printed in the UK by CPI Antony Rowe
Printed in the USA by Offset Paperback Mfrs, Inc

We operate a distinctive and ethical publishing philosophy in all
areas of our business, from our global network of authors to
production and worldwide distribution.

CONTENTS

Acknowledgements   vii
Introduction   1

Chapter One   10
Chapter Two   21
Chapter Three   27
Chapter Four   31
Chapter Five   36
Chapter Six   40
Chapter Seven   47
Chapter Eight   53
Chapter Nine   59
Chapter Ten   63
Chapter Eleven   68
Chapter Twelve   72
Chapter Thirteen   77
Chapter Fourteen   81
Chapter Fifteen   85
Chapter Sixteen   90
Chapter Seventeen   95
Chapter Eighteen   98
Chapter Nineteen   101
Chapter Twenty   104
Chapter Twenty-One: The Epilogue   107

About the Author   110

Books by Jim Young

(See www.creationspirit.net for descriptions)

Living an Extraordinary Life in an Ordinary Reality (O-Books)
2013! The Beginning is Here (O-Books)
Aware in a World Asleep (O-Books)
God's Pocket Dictionary
As if from God
On Making Love; Spiritual Testimony to the Gift Life Is
Real Life Leadership in a Newfangled World: The Essential Remedy for a Symptomatic Society
What If...? Changing Your Life to Fit Your Truth
Consider the Source: Rising Above Illusion Into the Light of Truth
Only Mind Matters: Emerging From the Waters of Symbolic Meaning
Keys to the Door of Truth
A Labor of Love: Weaving Your Own Virgin Birth on the Loom of Life
The Creation Spirit: Expressing Your Divinity in Everyday Life

Jim Young's Website: www.creationspirit.net

Available on Jim's website are additional creations and opportunities for expanding one's ability for living spiritually, including free downloads of talks and videos, speaking services and classes related to Jim's spiritual books, E-books and a link to his collector quality photography. Contact 1andrea.thomas@gmail.com to arrange an event.

Acknowledgments

I acknowledge inner guidance that has led me here. Indeed, Source has served me faithfully over time. I am grateful for the continual prompting that has led me to surrender to the calling of grace in Life. For this I give my all.

I give thanks for the book sent me by my friend, Siegfried Halus, which, by its format and design, spurred me on to shift the impact of this offering through an approach that was, until then, unfamiliar to me. Added gratitude goes to my friends—also authors—Marguerite Burgin and Nicolya Christi (contributor to my book, *2013! The Beginning is Here,* and author of, *2012: A Clarion Call,* A Wakeup Call for Humanity), for their editorial suggestions.

I give thanks, also, to several persons at O-Books: John Hunt, Publisher, who provided a steady and affirming hand in bringing this book to publication; Trevor Greenfield, for his diligent supervision of the publication process; Hayley Sherman, Copy Editor, whose remarkable editorial eye and sensitivity to deeper meaning has given literary and spiritual integrity to the final version; and Lee Nash, Designer, for so skillfully presenting this book in the best light. Singly, and as a team, these dedicated individuals have demonstrated their undying commitment to the highest quality publication.

I include in my thanks Gareth Strangemore-Jones of World ShiftMedia.org, for encouraging me to submit this book as an offering to be distributed through WorldShift's conscious evolution series. Thanks are also due to Jesuslaughing.com, for permission to use the graphic, Jesus Laughing, by Ralph Kozak (copyright 1977, Praise Screen Prints), for the cover image.

Last, and certainly not least, I give thanks for all those who continue to encourage and support me in giving myself to this form of communication about living spiritually.

Sincerely,

Jim Young

Introduction

Over the centuries, whether with the Bible or elsewhere, we have been led to believe that the teachings found in holy writ are to be taken literally. And that the information found there is historically correct and spoken as Truth to be followed—that Holy writ is the inspired word of God and thus infallible.

However, as we become more adept at moving from literal meaning and historical value to spiritual consciousness, we quickly begin to see that focusing only on the literal and historical aspects is to make ignorance manifest. This is not to deride other views of Truth. Ignorance speaks largely to unawareness—simply not knowing something; not being aware something in particular exists. Therefore, if people are ignorant about what symbolic meaning can bring to further under-standing, they can hardly be expected to have mastered symbolic meaning. The intention and substance of what follows is no different in its scope and meaning.

At the same time, giving people who are not yet ready for more sophisticated levels of understanding something far beyond their reach is like teaching higher mathematics to a baby. When people are ready for more, the time will have arrived for something more. Indeed, on a spiritual level, the time *has* arrived for something more. Experience tells me that people are now at a place in their lives where they are highly inspired to deal with life spiritually, instead of only intellectually and materially. Without doubt, the hue and cry for a more spiritual path is growing stronger and louder, and more and more people are dedicating themselves to finding deeper and more purposeful meaning for them. The good news is that a higher level of consciousness awaits our awareness and demonstration. Indeed, our conscious evolution continues, hopefully unabated.

We are largely ignorant of the value and use of spiritual

consciousness because we are stuck in the beliefs, opinions, false doctrines and erroneous agreements that have distracted us from spiritual Truth and instead landed us in the illusory world of duality. For many of us, being mired in the ego conscious realm has become our religious practice. Until we depart from expressing ego consciousness, we cannot reshape or reframe how we live and demonstrate Life from a spiritual reference.

Fortunately, more of us *are* hearing the inward calling spoken by the still, small voice beckoning us back home. The more of us who join the ranks, the quicker and more wholesomely we will demonstrate spiritual Truth. We are coming to realize that this inner spiritual calling is the only *authentic* calling we are to acknowledge and exercise. Each inward jewel of Wisdom we discern is a pearl of great price, costing nothing less than a full commitment to a better way—a simple but radical way of witnessing inner Truth. Radical times require a radically different approach, after all. Unquestionably, the more we adhere to the practice of The Inward Journey, the more we demonstrate being extraordinary in what has become a rather ordinary reality, no matter what outer appearance and authority say to us.

What you will find in the main text is one approach to parting the veil that blurs our spiritual vision and keeps us in a world of 'either/or.' The approach of which I speak utilizes the Bible as a series of allegories, a seemingly unending stream of stories that depict or lead us to Truth. Unfortunately, until lately, most of us have yet to be taught to read the stories for the Truth hidden there. Part of the reason the Truth is hidden is that we haven't found the key to unlock the means for doing so—seemingly, the key to the door of Truth has been hidden from us. I can assure you, however, that the key is not lost. The key has just been hidden, not by others, but by our relative inability to discern symbolic meaning.

The names of people found in the Bible, and even the locations cited, while designating specific people and places, *also* have a *mystical* meaning. The mystical meaning of every facet of holy writ can be revealed though the use of metaphorical, symbolic explanation, thereby defrocking the clothes of literality and ego conscious influence.

My purpose in this offering is to shed symbolic light on the spiritual teachings contained in the Gospel of John. I chose the Gospel of John rather than any of the other Gospels because the Gospel of John is written largely from a Gnostic point of view. Among other Gnostic views, some of which I do not ascribe to, the Gnostics taught that spiritual meaning comes not from literal understanding but from a deeper place, from heartfelt or inner knowing. The Gnostics called this knowing in the depths of our hearts, gnosis. I would call gnosis intuition, inspiration discerned—the Source of our Being—what it is, spiritually, that provides order to our lives when we become aware of and demonstrate only Source. As the sub-title of this book says in precise terms, all we need do is show up, listen, and then demonstrate.

If you follow this path of inward discernment faithfully, you are sure to find this same deeper resonance within you. You will come to know this deeper sense as Christ consciousness, the precious spaciousness having only highest good—conscious spiritual awareness and its demonstration—as its purpose.

In case you are not already familiar with the term metaphysics, I want to introduce metaphysics as the spiritual approach, the approach that marries the principles of spiritual awareness and divine order. The term metaphysics troubles many people, primarily because more is made out of its meaning and purpose than is necessary. To keep its meaning and purpose simple, metaphysics refers to what it is that brings spiritual order to our lives. Metaphysics thus refers to nothing physical at all—neither to intellect, belief or simple opinion. Metaphysics refers only to the still, small voice inherently available to all of us, and which, when faithfully abided, leads us to spiritual fulfillment—divine order—without reserve. In simple language, when living from the foundation and principle of spiritual consciousness, our life is perfectly ordered. This is the 'Be ye perfect, even as God is perfect,' Jesus admonished us to Be.

When we follow the guidance we find by becoming aware of what the voice of intuition discloses to us—heard inwardly as inspiration and enlightenment—we are demonstrating spiritual Truth to the planet. Contrarily, when we follow the guidance of outer authority—the vast array of ego conscious views that form duality—our lives are far more apt to be ordered by chaos, fear and feelings of lack. So our lives become chaotic, fearful and deeply lacking. Should we stay mired in the literal world taught by many of our forefathers, all we will have to guide us are the vast array of misperceptions and false teachings we see in our world today. And they will continue to breed a life of separation: from ourselves, from one another and from God—from Source, by whatever name. Hence, we fix ourselves firmly in a life of duality and call duality real—when Life is not that at all.

It is time to repent, to head in a radically new direction—a direction that takes us away from the illusory language and concepts that have misguided our lives to date. It is time to move toward the only real source of Truth for us, found inwardly. This is the approach taught through the spiritual language and allegorical teachings attributed to Jesus, as well as other mystics and poets before him and since. This is the example to follow—as well as the example for us to exemplify.

Treating Life metaphysically means that the only real lenses through which we have to view Life are the lenses of symbolic meaning that we find before us at any given moment. This doesn't mean that outer signs do not exist in and of themselves, or that outer signs are not valuable. What it does mean, however, is that there is *also* symbolic meaning for each of them, and this symbolic meaning speaks to us as spiritual Truth. When aware of this guiding principle, we use symbolic rather than literal meaning as the deeper guidance we need to fulfill ourselves spiritually. This is the spiritual meaning Jesus referred to when he said that if we wanted to know God we had to know God spiritually. We get to know God by knowing God symbolically—by looking at All That Is from a symbolic perspective. It is in this image and likeness that we can see the face of God and live—live anew, as never before possible.

Consider this: after dreaming during sleep, we often use symbolic understanding to discern the meaning and purpose of the dream for us. Using symbolic discernment thus makes us more aware of the deeper meaning hidden in the dream images. Sure, a dream is just a dream, but it also can serve to guide us from its spiritual essence. Likewise, it would enhance daily living immensely if we were to 'read' or discern Life in our waking hours in precisely the *same* way—symbolically. When we become more accustomed to 'reading' Life symbolically, we resonate with its Truth for us inwardly, and then Life is ordered by the spiritual intention discerned. Following literal leanings and reacting to appearance produces what most would classify as the ordinary reality found throughout most of our planet. Following inner callings generates extraordinary feelings of inner connection *and* the equally extraordinary quality of Life demonstrated into being by adhering to the spiritual guidance found inward, deep within our heart of hearts.

It is important to note at this juncture that nothing in this book is intended to discredit the actual life of the one called Jesus. What *is* suggested here is that it is *equally* important to comprehend that if we wish to live spiritually we need *also* learn to use the information available to us about Jesus and his teachings in a spiritual way, discerned symbolically.

The Bible tells us that Jesus came to life not to change Scripture but to interpret it. What follows is an interpretation—I prefer to call it an explanation—not unlike what Jesus brought to bear. What I am suggesting is a dramatic shift in perspective about spirituality. Our world of chaos and destruction—wherein we crucify others and ourselves daily—is quite the ordinary, very familiar to most of us. Yes, such ordinary living calls us to dramatic action, so we all may be resurrected to live anew—extraordinarily.

You need not be familiar with the teachings contained in the Bible in order to proceed, even though I focus on them for spiritual explanation. I will not be using the names and locations spoken of in Biblical Scripture directly, but simply as a reflection of what they contain. As you proceed, page-by-page, you will find Scriptural references from each chapter in the Gospel of John, as housed in the New Jerusalem Bible. These are used so you can have a frame of reference and contextual clues for comparing the Scriptural reference with the symbolic explanation. This book, like the Gospel of John, begins with the Prologue and ends with the Epilogue, sandwiching the remaining chapters in between the beginning and the end.

As you proceed, what you will be connecting with is the spiritual voice speaking from behind the mask of literality, speaking thus the intended spiritual tongue. Sometimes we feel like we're going through door after door after door to get where we see the light beckoning us, yet the journey is much simpler than what appears to be such a tedious trek. All we need to do is *show up*—and *listen*—focusing our attention on a new story, a story filled with the spiritual Truths embedded in the original versions. And then *demonstrate* our understanding of that story in—and as—our own lives.

Let this be our challenge: to eradicate ignorance, so we can come to understand and demonstrate the one and only Truth for us. Of this we can be sure: inward, we already have all we need to actively and authentically participate in this new way of Life. We only need to shift our perspective slightly, much like turning a kaleidoscope in order to obtain yet another form of beauty.

On these pages you will find what may appear to you as redundancy. Clearly, Scriptural revelation regularly reinforces in order to ensure a firmer grasp on spiritual reality, for most of us have a short spiritual retention span. When you turn the page to begin this version of a spiritual journey, I invite you to keep an open mind and heart. As long as you come to this version with an intention of spiritual awareness, you are sure to find you always have been spiritually aware, at least to some degree. It's only that the intellectual, literal approach—battered about in the fast-paced, chaotic world in which most of us live—has been a major distraction, and has hidden your spiritual awareness from view. When the smoke of unreality clears, you will see that spiritual Truth is waiting only to be made aware, just like every answer awaits the question that will reveal the Truth the answer contains. And duality will disappear as the illusion of our own making it is.

One admonition: the allegorical testimony provided reveals the extraordinary gift of spiritual discernment found in the teachings of Jesus. The spiritual explanation of Jesus' teachings shows us that allegorical testimony is not about Jesus, but about how to live with spiritual purpose and order, just as Jesus did. Living with spiritual purpose and order is the way Jesus referred to when saying, 'I am the way, the Truth and Life.' When taken spiritually, 'I am the way, the Truth and Life' takes us to deeper meaning: 'The way I am teaching you is the way Truth is found, the Truth that breathes Life into your being.' When we follow the spiritual way we can do what Jesus did—follow only Truth—and then we shall be doing precisely what Jesus did. Following inward Truth is what guided Jesus through Life. And he did wonders. Even greater than these shall we do, Jesus promised— as long as we abide The Inward Journey.

Keep this admonition in mind as you drink in what follows. Sip Wisdom ever so gently, savoring each 'aha' moment, each sense of enlightenment felt, and follow every inspiration as your purpose to be fulfilled. It's all just waiting for you to show up. So, by all means, show up, listen—and then demonstrate what it is you hear deep within.

These gifts of grace are found only in the present—in each moment of now. To be sure, the more ordinary life around us will be transcended by the Life of the extraordinary. Life will *become* extraordinary for you simply because *you will remember* that you *are* extraordinary!

Jim Young

What I must do is all that concerns me, not what the people think. This rule, equally arduous in actual and in intellectual life, may serve for the whole distinction between greatness and meanness. It is the harder because you will always find those who think they know what is your duty better than you know it. It is easy in the world to live after the world's opinion; it is easy in solitude to live after our own; but the great man is he who in the midst of the crowd keeps with perfect sweetness the independence of solitude.

Ralph Waldo Emerson
Self Reliant, an essay

The continuum of infinite, immortal Life is occasionally interrupted by a brief stroll into a body of highly limiting thought.

Dr. Jim Young

Chapter One

A: Prologue

'In the beginning was the Word:
the Word was with God
and the Word was God.
He was with God in the beginning.
Through him all things came into being,
not one thing came into being except through him.
What has come into being in him was life,
life that was the light of men;
and light shines in darkness,
and darkness could not overpower it.'

At the Source of any spiritually creative act or demonstration is our awareness of the voice of intuition, heard as inspiration, felt or experienced as enlightenment. Spiritually speaking, inspiration is the never-ending infinite Source being joined with its purpose—rendered as the demonstration of greatest good out into the universe. Intuition, the Logos, is the Word of God—the essence of our divinity—the Source that provides fundamental order of the cosmos. Spiritually speaking, the nature of inspiration is what guides us in its expression.

Nothing spiritual comes into being outside our awareness of this sacred Source. Whatever comes into being out of inspiration energizes and gives meaning to Life, making even the seemingly mundane sacred. Once embedded in the vast array of erroneous or ignorant ideas, we now suddenly experience enlightenment, and ignorance ceases to overpower spiritual reality in our minds and hearts. Indeed, out of darkness comes the Light—intuition, the still, small voice that enlightens us with deeper meaning. Infinite goodness awaits only our awareness.

The richness of inspiration, often called Wisdom, opens humankind to the vast realm of spiritual reality. Often we come to spiritual awareness or expanded meaning of spiritual purpose through a highly intellectual perception, but as yet not quickened by the Spirit, inspiration. Thus we have an intellectual understanding of spiritual Truth; at best, such renderings can be but signposts which direct us inward for the real—spiritual—awareness of deeper meaning. It is not through intellect that we are spiritually enlightened, but through the door of Wisdom. This relation between intellect and Wisdom, and the function of each, speaks to the archetype of consciousness that is not itself—but nonetheless leads us to—spiritual Truth.

Living in a world of domesticated understanding envelops us in others' beliefs, opinions, expectations, customs, regulations and laws; we are led by these distractions away from inner reality. It is little wonder that the still, small voice seems barely recognizable to us, let alone acceptable as a legitimate source of Being. Even so, recognizing our openness to spiritual possibilities makes for conditions that render the ground fertile for Truth, Wisdom's seed. It matters not whether we call this seed Truth, Wisdom, Source, God, intuition or inspiration, the Holy Spirit or Christ consciousness. In the spiritual realm, only our communion with this inner voice matters, not what we name the voice. Of this we can be sure: once felt, we know with absolute clarity these pearls of great price always have been, are, and always will be our only authentic form of spiritual intimacy and identity. They are wrapped in the brilliant Light or essence of the ineffable One and only. And we rest, finally, in our Holy Relationship with All That Is.

As we develop the capacity to listen inwardly for deeper, spiritual meaning, we come to hear the still, small voice some would call God. All else is a mistranslation of Truth. If we are to live an authentic spiritual life, our only purpose is to stay aware of the inner Source and then faithfully demonstrate its prompting out into the Universe. As long as we commit to living true to

Source, we are demonstrating the spiritual understanding that the Source and its demonstration are One—different in form, yet still One in image and likeness. Inspiration simply *is*, and thus it is *of*, *from*, and *with* the Source. Unquestionably, inspiration and Source are inseparable. By communing with the voice of inspiration—and never separate from it—spiritual Life is defined and fulfilled. There is no other way to live spiritually than this way, following this understanding. All that is required of us is to listen inwardly, so our True moment-to-moment calling can commune with our awareness, relentlessly applied.

Whatever comes into our spiritual awareness breathes deeper meaning into Life and quickens our Soul. Once enlightened, our unawareness—spoken of as ignorance or darkness—loses its power in our lives. The voice of inner Truth surpasses the voices of unawareness or ignorance as the real Source of spiritual meaning and purpose. Being 'true to myself' takes on the sacred meaning of heeding the whispers of the inner voice, which display themselves infinitely as gifts of grace. We are freed thus from the laws of agreement coming from the teachings formed in ignorance of spiritual Truth. Without doubt, as archetypes, mindsets or disciples of erroneous consciousness, these dimensions of intellectual and emotional bias cease to have power when superseded by Wisdom's government. In the wake of this newfound freedom, we come at last to see the face of God—not as some separate entity to which we must supplicate ourselves or petition—but as the voice of Wisdom, discerned as our communion with the resonance of inspiration, expressing enlightenment and demonstrating what we are always have been, are and always will be: divine.

B: Proclamation of the New Order

'"Who are you?" he declared, he did not deny but declared, "I am not the Christ." So they asked, "Then are you Elijah?"

He replied, "I am not." "Are you the prophet?" He answered,
"No." So they said to him, "Who are you? We must take back
an answer to those who sent us. What have you to say about
yourself?" So he said, "I am, as Isaiah prophesied:
"A voice of one that cries in the desert:
Prepare a way for the Lord.
Make his paths straight!"'

When we burden ourselves unnecessarily by asking who we are,
or who another is, we establish yet another curtain or veil
between our real selves and who we have come to believe we are.
We thus reinforce separation as a reality, when separation is not
reality at all. Who we are refers to roles we play, the illusion of
reality with which we paint our personality on the canvas of life.
We even feel the need to give our personality a name, like James
or Mary, artist or breadwinner. In the deepest meaning of
personal names, we find that these monikers refer to particular
dimensions of consciousness we employ while on this plane of
existence. These dimensions of consciousness are symbolic archetypes we play out in everyday existence. While seemingly
unimportant, just like the ego is thought by some to be, each
particular archetype serves as an additional signpost, an
important clue pointing the way back to our innate essence of
divinity.

This being said, the names of the twelve Apostles reflect the
archetypes we regularly face while on the human journey. We are
meant to become familiar enough with their characteristic
symbolism as to observe ourselves reflecting the characteristics
in our own behavior—as in others—using the characteristics as
cues to head us back to our innate essence of Being. These
characters, these archetypes of consciousness, are useful for
discerning what mindset we are using as the filter through which
we are viewing Life at any given moment.

As we become more aware or conscious of what filters we are

using to view Life, we also become more skillful at determining whether the particular filter or archetype we are employing is akin to the voice of Christ consciousness. If akin to Christ consciousness, we are to stick with it. If not, we repent—we change our perspective to reflect what we inherently know to be True. After all is said and done, Christ consciousness transcends archetypical definition and refers to the still, small voice we sometimes call God, whose only purpose is to guide us out of ignorance—back to our innate awareness of the Truth heard inwardly. It matters not what we call Truth, even though I prefer to call the path and its purpose—along with its demonstration—The Inward Journey.

We must be careful to comprehend the spiritual meaning of the term journey. Our spiritual journey is not about seeking something we don't already have. Such a definition would plant both feet solidly in ego consciousness. The spiritual journey represents our increasing willingness to become aware of what already is—and to live only there—as what we already are, have always been, and always will be: Divine. The journey and we become One.

To focus our attention more finely on discerning the aspects or dimensions of consciousness, we find, for example, that there is within us a facet of consciousness ever seeking to do right. Although reflecting a highly intellectual perception of Truth, this brand of awareness has yet to be quickened by the Spirit. Residing in this perspective, we are not yet in touch with the voice of Christ consciousness found only inward. Many of us reflect this archetype. As long as we adhere to its voice, we are liable to make only ignorance manifest. While having at its center a sense of peace reflecting a level of spiritual power, tempered with spiritual poise and confidence, in our domesticated state this archetype manifests as our natural religious tendencies—but not necessarily spiritual. In contrast, our natural spiritual tendency connects us inwardly with the still, small voice. When fully aware of such differences—sometimes subtle, sometimes not—we use our discernment of various archetypes to head us more properly inward.

Therefore, when discerning what dimension of consciousness we are abiding—should it be ego consciousness, for example—when asked 'Who am I?', if honest, we would respond with: 'I am not the Christ.' When abiding the religious but not necessarily the spiritual mindset, we do not reflect Christ consciousness. Instead, we reflect the archetype which points the way to Truth by establishing, with all who would listen, that there is a better way, a more spiritual way to discern Truth—and thus to demonstrate Truth.

Before going inward, we are not reflecting the unfettered power of the Christ. We have yet to learn that one cannot be in contact with the inner voice simply by zealously pursuing such clarity outwardly by ourselves, using primarily belief and opinion, intellect and rationality. These elements constitute duality fed by fear—ego consciousness, an external god's opposition (ego). This external god is the false idol we create in order to validate ego's primary characteristic, separation—and with it, all the opposition we can conger up to affirm duality as a reality. When we instead come into spiritual consciousness, we demonstrate the fullness of spiritual awareness by exhibiting the humble nature of a little child—letting the voice, the inner Source, speak from us out of innocence.

Neither does this shortchanging archetype represent prophecy, the foretelling of some Truth. When inhabiting the archetype reflecting an intellectual understanding but not spiritual intimacy, we would not be able to prophesize Truth, for we would have no real connection *with* Truth. When we are faced with the ultimate demand for the Truth of our existence, the best we can say in this form is that we represent what understands the real character of spirituality and fearlessly declares it. To arrive at our real identity we begin by transcending our body of beliefs, opinions and erroneous agreements. This act of transcendence acts as a purge, a purge revealing all forms of good as coming not from outer authority but through Christ consciousness—our highest self, the spiritual I Am. When making such a declaration, we are making the path to Truth one free of debris, one straight and narrow—and which is sure to deliver its promise of Truth to us.

Those seeking understanding in the outer signs give way to forms of religion—fixed ideas built up in consciousness through one's adherence to traditions, dogma, indoctrination and superstition—rather than gaining meaning and purpose through spiritual understanding. Many of us practice this archetype religiously, so it becomes the religion we practice. Those who think and live through this pharisaical archetype are bound to ask out of ignorance how one with an intellectual understanding of spirituality can help others cleanse their ignorance simply by pointing the way for them, instead of being able to tap the Truth for themselves. The obvious answer is to declare the simple Truth: just because we cannot exercise Truth ourselves does not mean we cannot point to the way that does exercise Truth.

To recognize that we are not yet capable ourselves—but yet can see a way that would make another, even ourselves, capable—is to actualize humility, a character trait to be admired and replicated at every turn. To say, 'I do not know,' is to set us on the inward journey, where only Truth is found. We cease functioning from the seat of self-importance and come to listen inwardly for Truth. When calming our turbulent thoughts and emotions, we ford the river of unconscious disturbance into the peaceful waters of Wisdom. Eventually, through spiritual cleansing of this kind, the fullness of spiritual awareness comes to rest in the harbor of Truth.

As we proceed through Life, becoming more and more aware of archetypical behavior and how it points to the voice or consciousness of the Christ, we see Christ, spiritual consciousness—the substance of this purer form of Life—restored to humanity by exercising The Inward Journey. The nature of Christ consciousness is to vivify all it touches, providing unceasingly and without restraint only the Truth of Being. When we sense Christ consciousness approaching inward, the simultaneous sense of Christ consciousness forever overcoming outer authority also becomes apparent. In this renewed state, we come to *know*—not just believe—that Christ consciousness does indeed take precedence over otherworldly states of consciousness.

Bearing the archetypical consciousness that points the way, we can declare our purpose with dignity. By pointing to The Inward Journey—even without ourselves yet being able to exercise The Inward Journey—we are fulfilling our purpose of Being. We are helping others cleanse themselves of levels of consciousness not at all useful in discerning inward Truth. It takes more than a washing away of our surface beliefs and opinions to ready us fully for spiritual Life. The deeper cleansing power of spiritual awareness—Christ consciousness—is necessary if we are to be fully restored spiritually. Our purpose in the exercise of Christ consciousness is to guide others toward deeper spiritual reality. As part of this realization, we also come to see that being quickened by the Spirit is like the dove of peace landing on our consciousness. The dove, landing as but a flutter on our heart, is a sure sign that we are cleansed and made ready for spiritual discernment by being in communion with Christ consciousness. Indeed, abiding Christ consciousness breathes Truth—and thus peace—into Life.

'The next day as John stood there again with two of his disciples, Jesus went past, and John looked towards him and said, "Look, there is the Lamb of God." And the two disciples heard what he said and followed Jesus.'

Other archetypes of consciousness also inhabit our awareness from time to time. As we come to Life pointing the way, we are sure to lead others to attributes of Christ consciousness that we see around us. When we do, we suddenly also become aware of other capacities or perspectives serving to color our view. When sensing—even when temporarily abiding another of these perspectives—our innate capacity and inclination for connecting with our natural state of divinity is not lessened. Actually, our capacity for spiritual clarity is heightened. Each time we find ourselves in the lap of an archetype appearing to be different from Christ consciousness, this awareness, like a bump in the night, casts us in the direction of Truth—if for no other reason than to become increasingly aware of our true Home. Even though we may not really feel at Home while exercising some other archetype—out of a sense of incompleteness or incongruity with Truth—on a spiritual level, we are at the same time enhancing our sense of Being at Home in Truth. Such is the giftedness—and the teaching power—of the other archetypes or dimensions of consciousness.

When we are open to the Truth, we are rejoiced greatly by finding Truth's inexhaustible source of power. By exercising spiritual awareness, we bond spiritual power with faith or conviction and—no matter what adverse circumstances confront us—we not only survive, physically; we thrive, spiritually. When knitting our innate spiritual power with our equally innate commitment to *demonstrating* such power, we are exercising Christ consciousness—inspiration made aware—into Being. This is the exercise of an unwavering faith in The Inward Journey, and the perfect verification of the power of the Logos. Unwavering faith in Truth is the rock of our salvation, saving us from other perspectives that obviate the path or way of Truth.

As the realization of Christ consciousness replaces the archetypes of personality—all those 'whos' defying spiritual reality—this spiritual cleansing inspires us to bring others to a similar awareness of Truth; indeed, to an awareness of the way *to* and *of* Truth. Surely, we will meet others who abide the archetype of one who is open to Truth and willing to consider ways of communing with Truth. This, like the embodiment of Christ consciousness, is the sign of one who is willing to increase in all phases of character, instead of engaging only with aspects of personality. Even so, there will be those who doubt any branch of archetypical residence other than their own as being fit for adoption or emulation. Surely, they think nothing different or unfamiliar could provide anything good for them. Nevertheless, when we are able to acknowledge that we are inherently connected to spiritual consciousness, we focus our spiritual eye on the form of worshipping Truth only. We become all the more receptive to inspiration as our way, our journey.

When confronted by the potential for spiritual deceit, taking Truth and distorting it as a reality, Christ consciousness allows us to look beyond deceit to acknowledge all emanations of Spirit as the perfection of Being. We arrive thus at the spiritual definition of beauty. Residing in the archetype of Christ consciousness, we see that there is no other meaningful translation or explanation of Life. Undoubtedly, when residing in Christ consciousness—innocent of erroneous translations—all else is but a mistranslation. Preceding the need to speak out in Truth—thus demonstrating the beauty *of* Truth—Christ consciousness informs us *as* Truth. Much like an acorn taking years to mature into a powerful oak tree, Truth, like the essence of true Love, is more than a thousand kisses deep, emitting the glow only Soul can impart—demonstrating Soul as only Soul can. Truthfully, beauty abounds.

When fully connected with Soul, we move out from Truth to inculcate it in others. Ironically, even though we connect with Truth and see its amazing potential for making those using other archetypes aware of Truth's value, our awareness is but the tip of the proverbial iceberg. Simply abiding conscious awareness is not the end of spiritual transformation for us. There is an even deeper path for us to abide: *transcendence*—the *fullness* of Christ consciousness becoming open to us once we are *wholly* committed. The full spiritual impact of The Inward Journey shows itself as infinite realms of inspiration, like the dove of peace, endlessly descending on us. Out of our unfettered commitment to demonstrate each inspiration faithfully, their image and likeness will descend on one and all alike. Peace fills— and joy abounds.

Chapter Two

'...the mother of Jesus said to him, "They have no wine." Jesus said, "Woman, what do you want from me? My hour has not come yet." His mother said to the servants, "Do whatever he tells you."'

The time comes in our lives when we have the opportunity to witness and participate in the wedding of the power center of consciousness with its demonstration. Until we do, there are but fleeting, but no less real, examples of the spiritual marriage heightening our ability to be spiritually aware. The opportunity for such an enlightened state usually arrives as we become more aware of the 'higher dimensions' of archetypical consciousness. Having witnessed the need for the dimension or archetype depicting the height of innocence, the ability to step outside the views of others, as well as our own—for those coming from spiritual consciousness—we are made additionally aware of the unfettered commitment to this complete demonstration of humility. Innocence commands authentic openness to another way—a fully spiritually conscious way—of discerning and exercising order in our lives.

The closely related dimension of unfettered commitment commands of us an undying, relentless, single-minded investment in the path of openness—surrendering to spiritual order for our lives. When abiding unfettered commitment, we would never entertain the notion of deciding for ourselves when to follow the tidings of innocence. Exercising innocence leaves no room for alternative means to Truth—The Inward Journey is the *only* way available. To entertain another way would be to mistranslate spiritual meaning and purpose.

In order for a wedding of innocence and its demonstration to be witnessed—to be complete, to be consummated—we must be in a state of consciousness which harmonizes with the inner revelation we call spiritual awareness. If we are closed to the possibility of something better for us than our own views, we will not become aware of the inner revelations coming out of innocence—the unceasing elementals of inspiration informing and spiritually guiding us to at-one-ment with the voice of Truth. When we are open to Truth, Truth comes into view, as one glorious revelation after another. Water is changed into wine; emotion is changed into spiritual reality. Without this harmonious relationship between heartfelt innocence and unfettered commitment to humility, there cannot be a complete union with Christ consciousness—Logos, the Word, spiritual awareness—which so powerfully and so perfectly orders our lives.

Should we be lacking the heightened sense of harmony required—the all-pervading essence of spiritual receptivity which sparks and enlivens the ultimate potential for a complete union—there is little hope of consummating the relationship. Indeed, it takes an abundance and clarity of harmonious intent to vitalize the means of bonding our intention with inner direction. When spirits are low, it takes only a reconstitution of commitment to shift the waters of limitation back to the deeper flow of vitality required for spiritual fulfillment.

Yet, when an uninformed capacity for completion attempts completion, living spiritually cannot be fulfilled. In order for completion or spiritual fulfillment to become a reality, we must be open to harmonizing humility with commitment. The commitment takes us to the Source, a mighty power, which washes away all the discordant elements and quiets our hearts and minds. We are then able to reduce everything coming to us to harmony and wholeness. The marriage of innocence with commitment is thus regularly honored and fulfilled.

All too often, we think all we need do is give faint inspection to our various dimensions of consciousness, just enough to intellectually understand them. To rest in this illusion is to take residence in a seemingly endless stream of superficiality, Life without soul. This is akin to the bride or groom having no real understanding of what it takes for a fulfilling marriage and thinking simply taking a vow will do the trick. The wedding vows go much deeper than sheer superficiality, a path lacking character or spiritual understanding. In order for a wedding with spiritual completion to be properly consummated — for water to be turned into wine — we must return, again and again, to the vitality of innocence witnessing to spiritual awareness — along with an *absolute* commitment to demonstrating the inspirational revelations arriving moment by moment. Our wedding is thus regularly consummated.

The very first sign of spiritual awareness is the bump in the night, making us aware of the need for a better way — and to faithfully exercise the better way in all facets of Life. We can then travel through Life exercising the healing virtues of innocence and commitment. In the process, any related mindsets are cleansed, and we transcend discord into spiritual harmony. By doing so, we provide the example of the natural healer through the workings of Christ consciousness. We, too, then, will have saved the best for last, for our time will have come.

'...he (Jesus) drove them all out of the Temple, sheep and cattle as well, scattered the money changers' coins, knocked their tables over and said to the dove sellers, "Take all this out of here and stop using my Father's house as a market."'

As we head toward inner peace through continuous realizations of spiritual power, we are tempered by the gradual cleansing of outmoded remnants of ego consciousness. Indeed, we are on the way to the attainment of peace the more we identify ourselves with the awareness of the Christ consciousness we are to abide. The more we identify with spiritual consciousness, the more we identify with the revelations our spiritual Temple contains and reveals to us. This enduring Temple we exemplify is built on the deeper understanding of Spirit or Christ consciousness as the only Source of order in spiritual Life. Along the way to this deeper comprehension, we meet the necessity to cleanse the symbols of ego consciousness, those archetypes holding beliefs, opinions, agreements, emotions and domestication among those which falsely order our lives.

At one time or another we come to ask: what is the currency of spiritual Life? Wherein is value found? The closer we come to the essence of the enduring Temple we represent, the clearer it becomes that the currency associated with spiritual fulfillment is not of the material world or its opinions and beliefs. The currency of spiritual consciousness is found in the deep recesses of the voice speaking only inward, which has only highest good—the currency of Truth, Wisdom—as its substance and intended demonstration. Coming to this awareness turns the tables on ego consciousness and duality and their focus on outer signs. By assiduously applying spiritual consciousness to the cleansing of the Temple, we cease using the Temple we are as a market for the currency of ego consciousness. Suddenly, we come into awareness of the archetypes having held us in ego consciousness and we cast them out, returning yet again to the sacred dimension of Christ consciousness. In no time at all, we find ourselves—there.

Unlike a physical structure called a temple—which, if destroyed, would take years to rebuild—all it takes to completely rebuild the enduring Temple of spiritual consciousness is the sudden awareness of Truth awaiting only our attention and acknowledgment. Through this awareness, the Temple is reconstituted in its original, ever-enduring form—instantaneously and completely. Remembering to be aware is all it takes on our part. The spiritual Temple is our only real body—the body of Christ consciousness—upholding Truth as the only currency to be honored and conveyed.

Our spiritual Temple is built and sustained by an equally

enduring commitment to the awareness and demonstration of each inspiration discerned. Each time the still, small voice is acknowledged, this latest insight or inspiration is brought to praise by laying it alongside the previous, and all which follow. Much like a physical temple, it gets built brick by brick, stone upon stone. The major difference between the physical temple and spiritual temple is the enduring quality of the substance of which the spiritual is made—and thus its capacity to quickly and completely regain its form once seemingly destroyed or tainted. Because our real Temple represents spiritual reality, its substance is of one kind only: the awareness of spiritual consciousness. The only way the Temple can be destroyed or taken from view is by lapsing into unawareness or forgetfulness. Yet it is immediately restored and made vibrant once again simply by regaining conscious awareness of the ultimate substance, the only authentic currency in this Life: the renderings of the still, small voice. We owe this way our very breath—that which is inspired, inhaled into existence—so we can just as powerfully expire it, exhale the breath of Life out into the Universe.

Of course, there are people who will try to enter their spiritual Temple without first fully cleansing their ways of all erroneous imagery. When this happens, they meet strong inner resistance, for they don't yet have the currency for correlating with the spiritual realm. Disharmony, dis-ease, is the result, and the Temple is at least tarnished by the erroneous attempt to enter. After all, certain conditions must be observed. One must be truly willing and open to the gifts of spiritual currency. When closed to these gifts, there will be no cleansing or making ready to enter the sacred Temple. The rubble of the outer cannot render the currency for entering the sacred inner realms without purification.

Purification is the vow we take when exercising our natural affinity for spiritual abundance. Without purification, the central vow is broken, and there is no way through the doorway to Wisdom. Each who wishes to take up residence within must make a 'burnt offering' of some kind, provide evidence of a sacrificial lamb of material thought or personal proclivity being purified through the fires of humility. This evidence witnesses one's commitment to regeneration of Spirit, and the door to the Temple is opened for the next and each succeeding step. Before we know it, the Temple we thought was only in the distant future appears before our very eyes without notice. Quite simply, once we adhere to the principle of spiritual currency, all the coinage is restored to glittering gold, and in no time at all our Temple is cleansed and readied for habitation.

Each of us is the priest or priestess of our own Temple, our own Kingdom of spiritual consciousness. When we enter with absolute commitment to the way of spiritual consciousness and its demonstration, we sacrifice the personal, ego conscious ways upon the altar of Truth. We then are rewarded by the eternal abundance found in the secret place of Christ awareness. We may not see the Temple in all its magnificence at first, but as we become more aware of the spiritual symbols feeding and nourishing us, we go deeper and deeper into the mysteries of Being—and our magnificence becomes more and more visible to us. In our commitment to The Inward Journey, we ascend to a place where the once seemingly mundane now appears as holy and complete in all aspects of Being. This is the beauty and continuity of our Spiritual temple once rebuilt—and how transcendence is defined.

Chapter Three

'"Rabbi, we know that you have come from God as a teacher; for no one could perform the signs that you do unless God were with him." Jesus answered:
"In all truth I tell you,
no one can see the kingdom of God
without being born from above."'

There is a dimension of consciousness which believes in the strict letter of holy writ and the ego conscious path, yet is open to a higher dimension if there is a sense it can be safely entertained. This dimension reflects faithfulness in the religious, while simultaneously becoming aware of inner, divine power. When witnessed this way, we have one foot in each camp and thus not fully in either. Even so, as we come to discern this particular mindset, we suddenly find spiritual consciousness producing very different—and greatly more satisfying—results than the ego conscious realm is capable of demonstrating.

By allowing ourselves to witness the spiritually conscious realm, we come to see we could not discern it regularly unless we first renew our perspective on Life itself. We come to realize the need to begin afresh, replacing the old mindset by cleansing the dysfunctional elements of consciousness with the purity and sure knowing of spiritual consciousness. By maintaining the mindset of ego consciousness, we will demonstrate only what this dimension can produce in the material realm. Just because we took on the religious context inhabited by those who came before us without really understanding its spiritual meaning does not mean we should stick with it. Sticking with ego consciousness would be to approach spiritual Life out of ignorance.

A contrary approach is called for; by regularly inhabiting spiritual consciousness we rest eternally in the lap of luxury, the

Kingdom of Truth, the infinite source of Wisdom, having only highest good in store for us. Spiritually, we must be reborn out of communion with the inner realm if we are to be spiritually complete and fulfilled. As a metaphor, the spirit speaks like the wind: we can hear its movement roaring into our awareness, but we cannot discern from whence it comes—other than inwardly— or specifically where it is going; only that it is sure to manifest in its likeness but not necessarily in the same form. This is the way the voice of intuition, Christ consciousness, speaks in us once we commit to the spiritual path.

Unless we are borne of this new perspective, we remain ignorant of its just ways in us. Although Truth speaks through conscious awareness of its inward voice, when not yet fully aware or still uncomfortable in its presence, often we reject the potential of its power in our lives. Even while catching glimpses of the benefits of spiritual awareness from time to time—largely because we habitually have followed the ego conscious way for most of our earthly lives—we reject the new until the old is completely washed away. Then, one day, while still being tempted by the ways of ego consciousness, we lift those ways up and we get the message that we cannot fulfill our spiritual heritage except through inward discernment of inspiration made aware. When followed faithfully, we provide example for others by walking our talk, which inspires and enlivens them to also walk their talk. The infinite voice of inspiration breathes Life into Being for one and all alike, so those who follow inspiration faithfully may overcome a life unfulfilled, and have eternal Life in its place.

The purpose of becoming aware of the hidden Truth is not to judge what is not Truth, but simply so those who become aware have a perpetual path of spiritual discernment upon which to tread. There is nothing judgmental about following The Inward Journey, but those who have yet to do so are actually judging the ego conscious way to be equal or even superior to The Inward

Journey. In this lap of unconsciousness, we are judging both our way and ourselves to be superior to the Truth found only within. We thus exemplify the vanity of vanities—resting in self-importance—instead of exemplifying enlightenment found only through spiritual awareness. Unfortunately, those of us who hide behind vanity—a belief in our separateness from Truth, from God—hide behind this false image or idol, thinking others won't notice. But thinking others won't notice doesn't even matter. What does matter is that whoever abides spiritual awareness lets enlightenment shine brightly, so others may clearly see the Source making enlightenment and transcendence possible.

> **'"It is the bridegroom who has the bride;**
> **and yet the bridegroom's friend,**
> **who stands there and listens to him,**
> **is filled with joy at the bridegroom's voice."'**

By being faithful to intuitional callings, we bring praise to the Source of them. Sometimes we give power to a way of thought, which approaches peace within us, yet still clinging to the relatively unconscious approach. While this incomplete approach is closely associated with spiritual Life and peace, it is not spiritual Life and peace itself. In order to get beyond our ignorant and unredeemed state, we must cross the muddied waters of sense concepts, which are turbulent with materiality. Our real baptism or cleansing comes when we extend ourselves beyond the unconscious and come to accept only inner Truth, spiritual consciousness, as our infinite Source of good. While our unconscious state can precede spiritual consciousness, the latter represents Christ consciousness itself, the inner voice speaking to us out of intuition, the womb of Wisdom.

As we found earlier, the inner voice and its demonstration are married, yet this marriage doesn't prevent those who are attendant to the power of this pairing—but not of it—from appreciating the sacred bond. This sense of appreciation is the inner pulse, the resonance with joy we feel when in the presence of this sacred bond of Truth and its demonstration. The purpose of this cleansing resonance—and our witness to it—is so the sense of appreciation can one day be replaced by the fullness of spiritual awareness. As this proceeds naturally, the voice of appreciation shifts dramatically to the voice of pure joy itself. The voice of joy is above all others and portrays a life of Spirit, while the sense of materiality it leaves behind could speak only of earthly things. Earthly things can fulfill us not.

While witnessing to transcendence, we know not everyone understands its witness or power. We know everyone does not accept the spiritual path. Nevertheless, those who do witness to Truth do so only because they have become aware of the still, small voice and are equally aware of its eternal and infinite power in their lives. They have come to comprehend that the fullness of spiritual demonstration lies in the hands of the intuitional voice, inspiring Truth into Being. The voice of intuition is where all spiritually authentic power resides. And when we abide our spiritual authenticity, all the rest is given unto us—eternally. Unfortunately, those who remain blinded by the ego conscious realm—and see Truth not—will know spiritual Life not at all, and will suffer from its absence in their lives. Either way, whatever we put out to sea comes back to us. Observing the return provides proof enough of the path we have chosen—and from whence it originally came.

Chapter Four

'Jesus replied to her:
  "If you only knew what God is offering
  and who it is that is saying to you,
  'Give me something to drink,'
  you would have been the one to ask,
  and he would have given you living water."'

The ego conscious archetype has us thinking we, who think we are so spiritual, are responsible for others following our example. When we step back from such a warped view, however, we clearly see it is those who have additionally come to honor their inspirational callings that most naturally spread the power of spiritual renewal. When the illumined intellectual understanding of spiritual consciousness is surpassed, we are more able to engage the inward Kingdom of spiritual reality. The disciples or facets of consciousness, the archetypes informing us of what perspective we are utilizing at the moment, come clearly into view when seen in the light of spiritual consciousness. When touched by enlightenment, the archetypes trend toward inner harmony. This is the natural procession of The Inward Journey.

As we head toward spiritual purification, we sense the mixed thoughts we have previously entertained. It is as though we have to work our way though them in order to get to 'the other side'. Yet, instinctively we know, simply by abiding spiritual consciousness—staying aware of intuition heard as inspiration—the mixed thoughts formerly feeling chaotic suddenly fall to the side of their own weight. Naturally, until we have reached this purer state of Being, we will have drawn our Life from the earthly side of existence. Nevertheless, we are destined—by the nature of spiritual existence—to draw a long draught of Life from deeper meaning, found eternally in the fount of inward Truth: the Living Water.

We thus ask inwardly for a drink from the spiritual realm, the flow of Truth that quenches our thirst for a better, more authentic means of demonstrating what we are called to Be in any given moment. Until we are clear in our declaration of this higher calling, however, our more limited view of spiritual consciousness is still colored and somewhat fixed on material ways and means. There is no spiritually clear view upon which we can yet draw. If we did have a clear view, we clearly would be asking for more, which would result in our being fed by a gushing, infinite stream of spiritual consciousness. When engaging others with this glorious prospect, we would do well to be prepared to respond to the natural inquiry about the source of our own Being. After all, if we aren't walking our talk, how could we legitimately expect others to faithfully follow our example?

As we engage with various levels of spiritual consciousness, we come to see with abundant clarity the ego conscious path leaving us in a state of unquenchable thirst for spiritual guidance. At the same time, we know on a deeper level that shifting directly and completely to spiritual consciousness itself does indeed quench our thirst. It is spiritual consciousness we are to wed, to join with. Living anew in this marriage, we are fed the living waters eternally, and without reserve. And spiritual intimacy arrives in the fullness of Love's embrace.

Still, again and again, we come across those remnants of yesteryear, the relation with a sense perception of Truth, which is not our real spiritual partner or soul mate. Christ consciousness, discerned through spiritual awareness, sheds light on all the sensory frailties thought to be true. As we become more enlightened, we see the ego conscious way attached to the various forms of outer worship, residing perpetually in the realm of the material, as dreams thought to be real. When abiding Christ consciousness, we are regularly guided past the illusory into spiritual clarity. We see spiritual consciousness dealing with the formless life and substance all the more clearly, and we are satisfied beyond belief. We are satisfied by our resonance with Truth heard and demonstrated and, henceforth, live faithful to Truth alone. Without further question, we know worshipping outer appearances and signs leaves us adrift, while worshipping the way of spiritual Truth grounds us spiritually and returns us to perfect ease with Life. Thus, dis-ease, as we've projected it onto the outer screen we call life, is removed as a lexicon of ego consciousness. This inner sense of satisfaction evolves into further understanding of this natural celebration of Life, which brings glory to the path itself.

As we exhibit our communion with the inner Source, others who are touched by this loving energy spread the word about the deep satisfaction it can provide. Eventually, they, too, come to understand our only spiritual purpose is to demonstrate this inner calling as best we can. Each demonstration is a stepping-stone leading to the grand demonstration, the collective merger with spiritual consciousness. Now we know it is not just because we heard of someone who witnesses to spiritual consciousness that it is true. As we witness the still, small voice ourselves, we can vouch for its perfection. Indeed, it is this spiritual awareness that saves us from ourselves, and not some man called Jesus, who claimed it not.

'Jesus said to him, "Unless you see signs and portents you will not believe!" "Sir," answered the official, "come down before my child dies." "Go home," said Jesus, "your son will live." The man believed what Jesus had said and went on his way home; and while he was still on the way his servants met him with the news that his boy was alive.'

Often, we get stuck in false representations of the loving Spirit. We provide pity and sympathy, solidifying the delusions of the sick by pitying and sympathizing with them and their claims of pain. Outwardly, we mourn and grieve, which only pulls down the sorrowful and grieving to meet the depths of sorrow and grief. Yet, when we uplift by praising and celebrating Life and completeness, all are elevated to a higher realm of consciousness. Such a spiritual acknowledgement simultaneously acknowledges an abiding compassion for harmony with the Truth of our Being, and we transcend all forms of discord, into harmony. This great soul compassion and yearning to help humanity out of its erroneous perceptions makes for natural healing. Indeed, we are healed when abiding Truth instead of fear-based duality. This is so because when we regularly reinforce the higher realms, the lower quickly disappear from view. The erroneous are healed through spiritual perspectives witnessed into Being.

When embedded in fear thoughts related to sickness or impending death, we obviate the more natural powers of humbleness and innocent receptivity—of inner Truth. When living out of inner Truth, we take on humbleness and receptivity—not as a *belief in them,* but as a sure *knowing of them* by *experiencing* them. Humbleness and receptivity then become a self-fulfilling prophecy in their own right. When we assist others in focusing their dark thoughts toward and about themselves, it only reinforces the apparent affliction or impending doom as a reality in their minds and hearts.

When we instead take the higher road—which is sure to cleanse the mind and heart on all levels—the resulting repentant intention reflecting a readiness to change one's attitude comes to the fore. The person formerly thought to have been afflicted comes to realize there is another realm where they can become aware of spiritual Truth, instead of focusing on the illusion of impending doom and gloom. This is grace, which saves us from ourselves—which saves us from our own, self-important ways.

By providing this cleansing perspective through our demonstration of spiritual awareness, we are witnessing to Christ consciousness, spiritual awareness. This ultimate form of enlightenment heals us of our many ego conscious wounds. The moral of this way of Life is that our body of consciousness is being robbed of its Life and goodness by the seemingly negating forces of earthly laws, beliefs and agreements, which hold us largely in a world of ignorance rather than enlightenment. The only way out is through the exercise of awareness, compassion and conviction, which are more in tune with the voice heard inwardly, and demonstrated in our everyday relations. Only then can we truly claim the title of 'Good Samaritan'.

Chapter Five

'...he (Jesus) said. "Do you want to be well again?" "Sir," he replied, "I have no one to put me into the pool when the water is disturbed; and while I am still on the way, someone else gets down there before me." Jesus said, "Get up, pick up your sleeping-mat and walk around." The man was healed at once, and he picked up his mat and walked around.'

As we head toward the consciousness of peace, we celebrate coming to greater realization that the more we abide this realm or dimension, the more we gain spiritual poise and confidence. On the way to this healing power of pure spiritual consciousness, though, we sometimes find ourselves slipping back, if not in physical form, then to the memory of the mindset which formerly crippled us. In the face of ultimate cleansing, we remember our previous commitment to the realm of ego consciousness and how it held us back; how living in duality distorted our view of Life and brought chaos, disrepair and dis-ease into our lives. Housed in this archetype, we placed our faith in the supposed healing power of ego consciousness instead of the swift and completely effective and efficient cleansing power of spiritual consciousness. Suddenly, when the greater realization came back into view, we became aware once again of spiritual consciousness being the natural liniment for all that ails us.

If ego consciousness is the bed we have made for ourselves, sleep in it we must. In such a state, we truly are asleep—asleep to the power of spiritual transcendence. How are we to awaken to the Truth of the matter? We head in another direction entirely: we pick up our lumpy bed we have slept in and turn instead to the path of spiritual consciousness. Here again, when we, the unaware one, place our dependence on the ego consciousness way, the multitude of illusions, uninformed opinions, beliefs and falsely applied agreements we have taken to be real hold us in place. They blind us to spiritual reality, cripple us from moving forward, infirm us with untruth. This is the bed we will have made for ourselves to sleep in. The good news is that we don't have to undo all these barriers in order to heal our erroneous patterns. The cement of illusion is broken simply by starting over again, making our bed anew, utilizing our inherently normal sense of spiritual devotion.

It matters not when or how we come to this righteous realization. The important thing is that we do arrive there—and we take the next step to further realization. The path is cleared for the fullness of spiritual cleansing simply by using any sign of slipping back into the ego conscious archetype or dimension to reassert the never-ending continuum of The Inward Journey. When we use the signposts of outer appearance to direct ourselves inward, the authority we formerly gave outer appearance, along with its demonstration, disappears from our arsenal of tools that hold us hostage. When we fail to use the outer signs to head us inward, we further cement what formerly crippled us, and we become even more embedded in ego consciousness than before. Sooner or later, however, we are called to abide spiritual or Christ consciousness as our natural Source, housed in the Temple of our own Being. We cast our bed of fear aside, and instead reside and walk in Truth. We rest, at last, in the bed of Wisdom, and fear no more.

To the uninformed, it may appear that by demonstrating spiritual consciousness out into the Universe, we are flaunting a means of achieving spiritual completeness. To those who are unfamiliar with The Inward Journey, and yet can see its benefits, anger coupled with envy would be a normal response. On some level, the angry and envious, too, want what Christ consciousness demonstrates. When faced with this reaction, it's good to remember that the response of others is none of our business. Our only business is living spiritually, no matter what the response of others.

As we declare our Truth—we of ourselves do nothing but follow the inner callings of intuition and inspiration. We witness The Inward Journey as the sole, and soul, journey of one who is aware of spiritual Being. And, as we know through experience, even greater than these will lead us forward on our spiritual journey. What breathes Truth into Life at the same time also breathes Truth into the Universe. Simply recognizing the Source lets us know the outcome is the same image and likeness, even if not in the same form. Just as simply, those who refuse to honor the awareness and demonstrations of spiritual purity are dishonoring the Source itself.

When living spiritually, we come to Life when living by the inner voice; our soul is ignited and we live in endless communion with the Truth for us. We are freed from what has deadened us to spiritual reality. Indeed, we have come alive! By living this way, we serve as examples for others to live similarly. They too will come to hear the inward voice calling to them; they too will reap the benefits of demonstrating their awareness. Along the way, we all become more and more facile and adept at spiritual awareness and demonstration. We discern easier and more quickly when we are about to stray from the spiritual path, and we become alive once again as we proclaim only spiritual consciousness as our way. We learn to judge not by word but by deed, whether or not we are following the inner calling to justice—the One and only way, spiritually, to righteous living.

As we walk this spiritual journey, we must remember that while we know spiritual demonstration simply by our awareness of its Source, there are those who as yet cannot discern this path, or even its loving demonstrations, for themselves. For these people, an outward sign is important: perhaps even someone to point the way to some outer sign. We who are spiritually aware do not depend on such signs, neither for validating the Truth they possess nor for salvation from our self-importance. However, we would do well to remember it wasn't too long ago that we, too, depended on outer signs—perhaps even on someone to point the way—so we should be gentle with those who function in a place on the spiritual continuum we ourselves once inhabited. Now, by the grace of inspiration, we are able to be both the pointer and the example, lighting the way and dispelling darkness. If we believe otherwise, instead of knowing Truth when we see it, the Truth will find no home in us, or—at the very least—we will not be at home with the Truth.

We would also do well to remember we once sought the meaning of spiritual Truth—Truth we could live by—in the literal translation of holy writ. Ironically, even though the literal meaning isn't the Truth itself, its symbolic meaning points to Truth without reserve. Because we were once ignorant of symbolic meaning found in allegory and metaphor, we refused to abandon our intellectual approach. Then, very suddenly, we heard a different drummer, a calling of a very different nature. By whatever means, we were awakened to the still, small voice speaking in another tongue, and we came to understand the tongue of Wisdom, Truth, as the only true Source of spiritual reality. We also realized all else is but a mistranslation of the tongue, which speaks the Truth of Christ consciousness.

Let us remember, then, to lead others to The Inward Journey by whatever means will best serve them where they are. If it's the pointer they are ready for, by all means reinforce this way for now, simply by pointing. If we can't put our faith in the ability of the pointer to show the way, neither can we give credence to The Inward Journey itself. After all, for many of us, it was the pointer which first brought us to where we now are on the spiritual continuum ourselves.

Chapter Six

'Then Jesus took the loaves, gave thanks, and distributed them to those who were sitting there; he then did the same with the fish, distributing as much as they wanted. When they had eaten enough he said to the disciples, "Pick up the pieces left over, so that nothing is wasted."'

While engaging spiritual insight, multitudinous forms of inspiration flood into our consciousness. Having seen the benefits of higher realms or dimensions of consciousness on our spiritual development, we give ourselves to even more. We act to commune yet again with spiritual consciousness, resting there with all our faculties. We cut off even the illumined intellect in order to come into closer contact with inner Source. Surely, as we 'show up' in earnest, we are fed the fullness of Truth's supply. The journey of passing over from lesser to greater spiritual consciousness is more fully engaged. Eventually, we come to comprehend there is no lower, and appearance found in duality is but a false witness to the idea that the lower also exists.

As we engage The Inward Journey, we look to release the power of highest good for the Universe and us. Through experience, we learn intellect and rational thought are void of spiritual Truth, a currency of little value, and thus lack the power necessary for spiritual cleansing, let alone transcendence. The voice of Truth, our awareness of spiritual consciousness, is the substance feeding us, nourishing the Soul. These seeds of spiritual substance represent the potential for spiritual completion—the ultimate magnitude of spiritual Truth. Should we be guided instead by the miniscule views of ego consciousness, our attempted conversion replicates those views. Believing we can 'fix' our views instead of transcending them, fixes us on misperception. We would have stymied the only one

Truth considerably, both in volume and intensity.

One thing is sure: the change we're dealing with here is huge by human standards. Spiritually, however, change is not what's required. What is required of us is simple remembrance of our divinity, coupled with a full commitment to The Inward Journey, the way of exercising our innocence and willingness to receive deeper meaning. The more we give ourselves to the intention and commitment to spiritual consciousness, the greater is our source of abundance and its demonstration on all levels of Being. Even in view of this powerful means of spiritual demonstration, some view the intellectual experience and outer signs and mistake them for a higher form of spirituality. Energizing intellectual treatment only spiritualizes ego consciousness—spiritualized ego consciousness is not spiritual consciousness itself. Erroneously, some still clamor for the appearances of the ego conscious way, instead of realizing the depths from which spirituality comes, and abiding the means of resting in the depths. No matter what the outer perceptions of others, it is ours to flee the old dysfunctional patterns and instead abide the inward journey. Surrendering to Truth is what takes us there.

'...they saw Jesus walking on the sea and coming towards the boat. They are afraid, but he said, "It's me. Don't be afraid." They were ready to take him into the boat, and immediately it reached the shore at the place they were making for.'

As we come to exercise compassion for others and ourselves by living True to the inner calling, this powerful conversion releases the virtue that transcends all inner discord—all those erroneous beliefs and opinions—and we arrive in harmony. We are led thus to serve as examples for living beyond the stormy seas of self-inflicted doubt and fear. When still partly focused on past practice—exercising various realms or dimensions of ego consciousness—those elements serve to toss and turn us in the stormy seas, erroneously thought to be life itself. Ego conscious thoughts do indeed form a stormy sea, one requiring faith placed in a different source in order to navigate it more peace-fully—the Source found only inward. A fuller comprehension of the power and character of spiritual consciousness causes us to exercise our faith in ways which overcome day-to-day emotional storms. In the ultimate form of spiritual consciousness, we come to see that it is not faith, but the sure inner knowing of Truth, Wisdom's way, that quiets the emotional waters.

The majority of us live in ways that we have come to believe are better at controlling our lives. Stuck still in the more super-ficial dimensions of duality, we demean the more spiritual means of coming to peace, and so we often sink in the troubled waters—deep-seated emotions—permeated with fear and its unsavory 'cousin', doubt. From this substandard vantage point, we see the saving grace of spiritual discernment as but an apparition, a phantom, a weak and empty alternative, when quite the opposite is correct. Eventually, perhaps just when we fear we are about to drown, we are awakened to the inner voice, commanding our full attention to spiritual comprehension and its demonstration. And we are saved, standing now on sacred ground.

Sure enough, by adhering to spiritual consciousness, we come to see all the discordant dimensions of thought being quieted, and we walk on in peace. From then on, everything our newly found sense of inner peace touches is reduced to harmony and wholeness. Spiritually speaking, we then can walk peacefully on troubled waters. Primarily, we can walk on troubled waters because the troubled waters are not real. The troubled waters represent only the various illusions of fear. Only Christ consciousness is real. When we walk in Christ consciousness, fear is seen for what it is: unreal, a nightmare thought to be real, and not to be taken seriously. We would do well to laugh at any suggestion that we do take it seriously.

'Jesus answered:
  "In all truth I tell you,
  you are looking for me
  not because you have seen signs
  but because you had all the bread you wanted to eat.
  Do not work for food that goes bad,
  but work for food that endures eternal life,
  which the Son of man will give you,
  for on him the Father, God himself, has set his seal."'

We falsely travel from one dimension of consciousness to another, hopefully, deeper and deeper. The Truth of the matter is that we need neither cleanse nor travel to one dimension before heading to another dimension. We only need to become aware of the One and only dimension: spiritual consciousness. Awareness is about trading in a *belief* in alternative dimensions of consciousness for the inner *knowing* of the one and only, spiritual consciousness. Belief holds us in duality and limitation. Belief holds us in the dimension of thinking there are differences to conquer in the spiritual realm. Once focused inwardly, however, we come to the realization, the awareness, that there is no real alternative to the Truth speaking to us in apparent difference, separation. This realization includes the awareness that *we* are the Temple, and hold *only* Truth.

When stuck in the illusion of ego consciousness we have created, we come to a faint conclusion that the illusion has somehow turned us in a more spiritual direction, and we are ready for more, and from a very different Source. This apparent shift, much like the signposts of outer appearance, points to the Truth, but in and of itself it is not—cannot be—Truth itself. Actually, it is not the outer appearances inspiring us to want more, but rather the inner resonance with Truth calling us *to* Truth. Once felt, we simultaneously comprehend that we are not to search for Truth in the ego conscious realms, formerly thought to be true and righteous. Clearly, abiding ego consciousness is no longer an option for us. Once Truth is seen for what Truth, Wisdom, is—the One and only divine Source—the illusion seen as some other source disappears from view. Illusion is created by assigning our limited perspective—rather than Truth—to Life's offerings. It's not that some appearance is not real; it's that we apply our limited understanding rather than letting Truth identify the appearance for us. Other dimensions are only a figment of imagination, governed by fear.

Interestingly, along the journey to awareness of the One and only, we often hear, even express ourselves, the hue and cry for a description of God's work: What is our purpose as a spiritual Being? Sitting in our more natural state of spiritual consciousness, we discern with inescapable clarity our only purpose: giving ourselves to the awareness and demonstration of each and every intuitional, inspirational, enlightened rendering heard inwardly. We don't need outer signs to guide us when we give ourselves to the demonstration of each Truth discerned. Focusing on Truth, and this focus alone, constitutes our purpose of Being. Focusing on manmade laws and both collective and individual beliefs of mankind does not—cannot—deliver inner peace. Nor do they nourish us spiritually. The only true nourishing Source is the voice of our highest Self, and we are enriched and nourished beyond measure by delivering the commands of this voice as we become aware of them.

Time and again we hear inwardly that we have but a single purpose. Still, from time to time, even when we know only Truth is being delivered—because that's all that Truth *can* deliver—we are tempted to maintain our belief in outer signs and hold them to be the true indicators of spiritual living. If we give in to the temptation, all we can manifest is a likeness of its source: yet another form of ego consciousness. By maintaining our focus on our spiritual purpose and the voice of its Source, we discern that *everything* coming to us as inspiration is to be demonstrated, and thus is fulfilled. Not a single inspiration is to be cast away simply because it seems too small or too insignificant to merit our full attention. Just like miracles, there is no difference between the small ones and the more obvious. Each miracle is a miracle—period. Just as in miracles, each inspiration is the spiritual norm, not something exceptional that is to somehow wow us. Each inspiration simply is—and is thus to Be. It is our purpose to demonstrate Being faithfully, without reserve or special favor. Demonstrating each inspirational motivation is precisely what honors inspiration, dignifies inspiration, and praises inspiration *through* demonstration, each as only we can. To be sure, it is demonstration, and not merely words, which expresses gratitude in full measure.

Such dedication sometimes disturbs those who are unaware of spiritual purpose. Ironically, many who are inadvertently or by design put off by the display of inspiration in such a seemingly effortless manner actually often engage inspiration in a similar fashion. It's only because they have bought into the ego conscious means of living that the more spiritual seems to be missing in their lives. So, in a very real way, anyone who has listened inwardly and become aware of the power of inspiration will be drawn increasingly towards inspiration. The example we set by our own demonstration heightens this awareness in all touched by it, even if only as a seed dropped or as a whisper speaking like the wind stirring the Soul. The connection with the resonance we feel as Truth lets us see the face of God—the face of inspiration prompting us to its fulfillment, and ours. And our wills become One. Contrary to the erroneous translation of Scripture, we *can* see the face of God and live—we can just never live the same way again. Once we imbibe the sacred drink of Spirit, we know we are to dedicate ourselves singly and completely to Spirit and its fulfillment.

The voice of inspiration is our only real nourishment on a spiritual level. Inspiration is the bread of Life. Inspiration breathes Truth into Life and forms the foundation for and of The Inward Journey. Inspiration is the flesh and blood that gives Life to the world of saints. Each of us is this saint, waiting only to become aware. In this way, the inspirational food and what its Wisdom becomes are One—different in form, but still the exact image and likeness of the originator, nevertheless. Wisdom awaiting awareness and Wisdom demonstrated or fulfilled are both forms of Wisdom, are they not?

From this, we can deduce that Life forms the foundation of spiritual consciousness, and converts those who are aware from being static, to Being fully alive. We thus come to know that there really is nothing but inspiration feeding us, nourishing us, and bringing us to Life in the most powerful ways. We know ego consciousness cannot fulfill us—only inspiration can and does. Inspiration and ego consciousness are worlds apart. After all, Inspiration is the Word or voice of Truth, guiding us faithfully in the spiritual realm—announcing ego consciousness as but a form of fear we make up in order to avoid spiritual awareness. Just like the past and the future, ego consciousness does not really exist, so should either be ignored or used to our advantage whenever it, in any of its many forms, appears.

There is a complete arrangement of conscious dimensions we find as we head towards the only one True dimension. The appearance of others can serve to show us the value of appearance as a general rule: as reminders to return to spiritual awareness. At the same time, we come to see ego consciousness as what betrays the Truth of the matter. The only matter—the only substance of spiritual Life—is inspiration made aware and demonstrated into Being.

Chapter Seven

'Jesus said,
   "My teaching does not come from myself:
   it comes from the one who sent me;
   anyone who is prepared to do his will,
   will know whether my teaching is from God
   or whether I speak on my own account."'

As we travel into higher spiritual realms—higher forms of consciousness—we find our journey taking us into the practice of more frequent connections with Truth found inwardly, and with dynamic spiritual energy bringing into light the disciples, faculties or archetypes of humankind. When in the Kingdom of Heaven—this deep connection with Christ consciousness, Truth—we often see, in their exposed state, the necessity and opportunity for dropping these disciples of error from our repertoire of archetypical behavior. When engaging with the transcendent manner of spiritual living, parts of the contrasting imagery of archetypical consciousness would, like the ego conscious realm it represents, want to do away with our higher levels of being, for fear of being replaced. The good news is, while in the abode of Christ consciousness we clearly see we need not be afraid of other competing levels of consciousness. We come to realize that there is only one real form—spiritual, Christ consciousness—which is the Truth we are to demonstrate. Spiritually speaking, there is no other alternative.

The disciples of archetypical consciousness would only naturally wish us to be drawn into their lair, rather than staying in Christ consciousness, where they would be exposed to the possibility of transformation and transcendence themselves. Our archetypical orientation, a common human element of deceit and deception, would naturally want to defend itself, even to the point of wishing to expose embedding ourselves in Christ consciousness as something to be overcome. This is the normal sense we have about doing battle during this total immersion in Christ consciousness. The last remnants of opposition fight for their lives using every tactic possible, including injecting a sense of impropriety, a lack of faith, and untoward secrecy into the mind. These ploys also inject guilt and shame for remaining in our inner realms of consciousness, rather than exposing our deeper sense of spiritual awareness out into the open, where it would be easier to attack by contrary views.

From the ego consciousness point of view, it would be better for us to put ourselves on display at all times along the way, where any counter forces or contrasting viewpoints would have a better chance to attack. While residing in Christ consciousness at higher and higher levels of frequency, however, we realize old tendencies are overcome not by external exposure of our newfound spiritual commitment, but by more fully assimilating the commitment and process of complete connection—at-one-ment—with Christ consciousness. Therefore, we do not expose ourselves to outer reaction prematurely.

Even so, as Life is being celebrated—or barely lived, depending on one's perspective—those at varying levels of spiritual commitment naturally wonder about how one who lives in the fullness of Christ consciousness demonstrates this level of being. While imagining it for themselves—operating out of various archetypical patterns of their own—others most naturally see The Inward Journey of adhering to Christ consciousness as making one a good person. Those of a more suspicious and distrusting archetype would think they are being led astray by the suggestion that there is only one real way to the Kingdom of Heaven. Just as naturally, most would keep their views to themselves—at least until they committed one way or another—not wanting to expose themselves unnecessarily to the criticism of non-believers.

'Then, as Jesus was teaching in the Temple, he cried out:
"You know me and you know where I came from.
Yet I have not come of my own accord:
but he who sent me is true;
You do not know him,
but I know him
because I have my being from him
and it was he who sent me."'

Once we have assimilated the practice and substance of living in the fullness of Christ consciousness, we begin to step out in this fullness of spiritual discernment. Indeed, our time will have come — and we begin teaching by example in the halls of everyday living. As we enter this realm of example, others will wonder how we came to be so versed in spiritual demonstration. They didn't see us studying about Christ consciousness, or even know of our contemplation about the path of at-one-ment. We then will respond by saying: 'Christ consciousness is not something we find in books or that I have made up myself. Christ consciousness is found only inward, by making a commitment to going within for all spiritual guidance. Anyone who has also made the commitment to live by Christ consciousness — and this alone — will know our example comes from within us, from listening for the still, small voice, and not as any figment of our own construction. When speaking from ego consciousness, from self-importance, we seek the path of self-aggrandizement. While honoring Christ consciousness, however, we honor the fullness of spiritual integrity. Even when defining Christ consciousness as the spiritual path (law) to follow, most, for obvious reasons, are reluctant to follow the spiritual path. There is a process of increased awareness required before moving on comfortably, let alone lived as a full-fledged spiritual commitment.

When in this position of teaching by example, such spiritually pure teaching engenders contrary views in others. Whenever others are faced with a Truth contrary to their own grasp on life, they become unsettled, uncomfortable, even angry. They often want not only to defend their own views, beliefs or opinions, but on some level—out of fear—they even consider killing the messenger who raised the spiritual counterview by example, not literally but figuratively. Rather than stopping to consider the possibility that another perspective on Life might indeed be more compelling, they defend their misperceptions to the hilt. Living by the misperceptions of appearance, they fail to avail themselves of deeper meaning and purpose. All those who are fully committed to The Inward Journey commit to its demonstration another way—a way which steps away from self-importance and self-righteousness—a way which emphasizes the fullness of humility, going inward to a higher Source for one's spiritual guidance. And yet we find those who regularly practice highly erroneous ways of conducting life—many ways—wanting us to cease the one single practice that informs our entire spiritual presence.

Even so, there are those who stand by the wayside, with no particular practice of their own, who are willing to consider the potential for something better. When they see no one having any real counter to the example of Christ consciousness lived, they may properly conclude that there *is* no real counter to the Truth. Although they may know who this person is who lives by the example of Christ consciousness, however, they also know they cannot yet fathom the Source itself. When living this example, we naturally respond from the seat of Truth about Christ consciousness: 'You may know me and where I come from, yet I have not come from my own accord, but from the guidance found in Christ consciousness—the only Truth we are to follow. You who do not follow Christ consciousness would have no idea what Christ consciousness is, let alone the endless trail of spiritual guidance it provides. But I do, because I have committed my Life fully to following Christ consciousness, which sends me, endlessly, on my way.' Still nonplussed by the strength of character and level of Truth heard, those in opposition wait in fear of contradiction.

When we lead by example there are some who *are* taken with the possibility of a better way, who *are* willing to move forward — if only they had a few more signs to bolster the courage of their convictions. Yet, the sign we have to give is but a single sign: to live our commitment to Christ consciousness by example. While those who oppose us may well want to shove us aside or put us away, unfortunately even those who are able to see the potential of another way — but not yet courageous enough to go within for spiritual guidance as their own way of being — will not be able to connect inwardly. Because of their lack of commitment — or high level of fear or distrust — they are not yet able to find the inner connection that is best taught by example.

> '...Jesus stood and cried out:
> "Let anyone who is thirsty come to me!
> Let anyone who believes in me come and drink!"'

What will we leave those who, as yet, cannot bring themselves to fully commit to The Inward Journey — to living an extraordinary life in an ordinary reality? All we can do is to continue teaching by example, so those who thirst for spiritual Truth can find the way — and have the same fount of Christ consciousness to drink from as we do. Without doubt, future followers will come to taste the incomparable draughts of Spirit, which flow from the heart of hearts, our Truth of being.

Many are left in a world thriving on quandary: an inner dissonance with Truth, but only because they are not yet familiar with the way or voice of Truth. When unfamiliar, we sense an inner connection of some kind when we resonate with the Truth demonstrated in word and form, and yet we think — out of our pattern of domesticated belief and opinion, the rational, literal means of determining the laws we live by—that the Truth should come from some objective judgment, not spiritual discernment. Surely, Truth must be objectively verified or it is not Truth at all. Only one bereft of spiritual discernment would level such a charge; one who has adulterated him/herself by a commitment to the erroneous ways of this world, the world of ego consciousness and its imposition on our lives. But there is always the opportunity to go beyond adulteration, given the infinitude of each single moment of now, which opens the door to starting Life anew all over again.

Chapter Eight

'Jesus again straightened up and said, "Woman, where are they? Has no one condemned you?" "No one, sir," she replied. "Neither do I condemn you," said Jesus. "Go away, and from this moment sin no more."'

While others go on their merry way, mostly oblivious to their natural divine state, those who are fully committed to The Inward Journey give themselves totally and single-mindedly to a state of spiritual realization. The spiritually oriented give themselves to the inner connection and demonstrate inner connection by example. Along the way, others are attracted to such enlightened beings. They may not even know they are attracted, yet many who are touched on some level of being gravitate to the lap of spiritual enlightenment.

Sometimes, such 'visitors' to the more enlightened learn by watching what happens when someone who is accused of being 'less than' or 'not good enough'—a 'sinner', so to speak—is treated by the enlightened. Such opportunities for learning about one's spiritual integrity can serve to light the path of personal redemption. The more we practice spiritual discernment, the more aware we become of the Truth it renders and, as is most often the case, we are tested—or so it appears. For example, we may find ourselves being confronted with a situation where others want to see how we would treat another who seemingly has adulterated him/herself to something other than a full commitment to Christ consciousness. This is a good example to consider, holding true to the voice of Christ consciousness by going inward for guidance.

If we were to respond like those who are testing the sincerity of our own commitment, we might well respond by saying the one who is not fully committed has indeed sinned and ought to be punished. Those who still do not see others and themselves as divine often cast stones of aspersion at others. Of course, to do so would be to miss the spiritual Truth entirely, for as we cast aspersions at others we are only denying our own level of prostitution. We prostitute ourselves to separation, failing to see we denied our own divinity by accusing another of also lacking divinity. Divinity is permanent and unchangeable, no matter what the outer appearance, no matter whether someone is able to acknowledge being divine, or not.

On the other hand, when using our natural acuity for spiritual clarity, we would see such a person—no matter what the appearance—as perfectly divine. It may well be that he/she has simply forgotten that he/she *is* divine, so how else *could* he/she behave when memory is challenged? The sum and substance is this: anyone seeing someone as less than the perfect light of spiritual completion would also be prostituting themselves to such a diminished view—whether it's about someone else or themselves.

What are we to demonstrate here? Quite simply, we demonstrate our ability to turn ourselves completely around—to repent—and go inward to find and connect with the still, small voice of Wisdom. When in the seat of Wisdom, we refrain from being judgmental towards someone—including oneself—and from missing the mark of perfection found in our innate divinity. The larger demonstration is to practice remembering *what* we *really* are—divine—and to demonstrate only our divine nature out into the world, sinning thus or prostituting ourselves no more. When we turn ourselves around this way, the forgiveness we think we need from others and ourselves is rendered unessential. Obtaining a new perspective—as one bathed in spiritual discernment—we come to Truth about ourselves, which, in and of itself, *is* forgiveness. The old perspective is for giving up and thus for getting on with Life—and living only Truth. As long as we walk the path of commitment to Christ consciousness, we will not be living in spiritual ignorance. Indeed, we will form our lives only from the seat of enlightenment.

> 'Jesus replied:
>   "Even though I am testifying on my own behalf,
>   my testimony is still true,
>   because I know
>   where I have come from or where I am going;
>   but you do not know
>   where I come from or where I am going.
>   You judge by human standards..."'

Those who look askance at someone living from a spiritual base are wont to say such persons are living a lie, simply because the spiritual example is so contrary to what the critical voice is accustomed to seeing and experiencing. The powerful vision of spiritual integrity makes others feel uncomfortable in its presence, so as to encourage criticism and either ignorant or naïve inquiry. Spiritual clarity testifies to itself by demonstration, thereby validating Wisdom, Truth's awareness. Those who are not spiritually aware see Life from a different perspective— through a glass darkly—having erected a veil of ego consciousness between themselves and the spiritual Truth. The less spiritually informed are quick to judge someone for being different than they are—and most likely, less than holy, as they hold themselves to be. However, just because they could find validation of their claim through corroboration with others like themselves, this form of judgment would not necessarily make their claim correct.

When living out of Christ consciousness, not only does the demonstration testify to spiritual awareness, but the deeper sense that the demonstration comes from the divine inner Source also testifies to its validity. Although there are two witnesses, one witnessing to demonstration of Christ consciousness, with the other witnessing to the holdings of ego consciousness, those who are not familiar with the face of enlightened demonstration are also unfamiliar with the Source generating the demonstration. The currency of the spiritual domain is Christ consciousness made aware and demonstrated, rendering the currency of ego conscious demonstration completely bankrupt.

Some of those who can't quite yet bring themselves to commit to The Inward Journey—but still desire to do so—will look to the more spiritually aware for guidance. However, because those of the ego conscious orientation look for outward validation or guidance, they naturally fall short of spiritual completion. Only the power of the inner voice can provide spiritual clarity, and those who look to the outer have yet to know how to hear the inner voice. Living by the inner voice is the only source of spiritual fulfillment, and such a commitment is not the way of the ego conscious commitment or affairs. If those who live out of ego consciousness do not change their perspective, the opportunity for living spiritually is dead—at least until and unless they do change their perspective.

'To the Jews who believed in him Jesus said:
    "If you make my word your home
    you will indeed be my disciples;
    you will come to know the truth,
    and the truth will set you free."'

Taking hold of the Word of Christ consciousness makes one a disciple of Truth discerned. To know and practice demonstrating the Truth makes us free; free to Be what we truly are—divine— instead of what we have come to believe we are—something less than divine. We must be careful to comprehend that Truth itself is not what makes us free. What makes us free is the *knowing and demonstration* of Truth. For when we commit fully to knowing and demonstrating Truth, we are freed from the grip of ego consciousness. Just how do we know something is the Truth? Knowing Truth, we feel free—free to demonstrate *only* Truth. At this very instant we know there is nothing *but* Truth to know and demonstrate.

When we retain the ego conscious viewpoint, we enslave ourselves to all that ego consciousness manifests: a world governed by fear, chaos, manipulation and self-importance. Such manifestations offer testimony truly to a world of duality, formed out of a belief in separation—believing we're separate from one another and all of life—separate from God, separate even from ourselves. This foundation of separation rests on a supreme testimony to vanity: it is supremely vain to think we are separate from anyone or anything. The only way to be freed from this kind of enslavement is to acknowledge its disarray and then to focus on Truth. Yet, acknowledgment is difficult as long as the uninformed believe their heritage is based on the foundation of ego consciousness, even if they don't know the foundation *is* ego consciousness.

Living out of ego consciousness means we live from self-righteousness and self-importance and we get what we *think* we want, so we stick to this pattern out of familiarity and comfort. We abide ego consciousness and stay stuck in its disastrous results. This ego consciousness outlook murders the Truth, for it keeps a veil between the Truth and us, so we are oblivious to Truth's power in our lives. The more we practice ego consciousness, the stronger ego consciousness becomes a habitual commitment to something having no awareness or connection with Christ consciousness at all. Ego consciousness, duality, has no grounding in Truth, only in the illusion we erroneously make of Life. Therefore, it can witness only to illusion. Certainly, ego consciousness cannot, does not, witness to the Truth found in spiritual awareness and demonstration.

Ego conscious law has no relation to the ways of spiritual discernment and demonstration. When we make ego consciousness, duality, the god we follow, we bear false witness, and have constructed a false idol we worship. And we say we must solve the paradox attributed to such an erroneous juxtaposition. Make no mistake about it, our religion is defined by what we commit to day-by-day through our demonstration. What fathers our heritage, from Abraham on down, is inner knowing, the conviction that fulfills our only true nature through spiritual discernment and demonstration. The truth is that the voice of Christ consciousness is the eternal voice, having neither beginning nor end. Christ consciousness is the voice of Wisdom, eternally and infinitely available to those who have ears to hear and eyes to see—spiritually. Abiding spiritual commitment protects us from the distractions and judgments housed in an ego consciousness foundation. No longer do we prostitute ourselves, knowing there is only One—nothing but One.

Chapter Nine

'"Neither he nor his parents sinned," Jesus answered, "he was born blind so that the works of God might be revealed in him.

"As long as the day lasts
we must carry out the work of the one who sent me;
the night will soon be here when no one can work.
As long as I am in the world
I am the light of the world."'

If we're walking on the spiritual path, by now we understand that the term 'cure' refers to how one's views of life have changed. 'Cured' does not refer to some physical healing, as when, literally, one who is crippled is now healed. When in Scripture we see someone is born blind, spiritually this means the person spoken of is using an illusion to bring order to Life. Illusion is not real—because only Truth is real—so how could illusion bring order to anything, let alone Life? The only way this could be so is if someone is using illusion as his/her reality—substituting one's personal perspective for the Truth of the matter. Truth be known, when we live—demonstrate our lives—out of ego consciousness, the beliefs and opinions we maintain are what determine how we define events, circumstances and people for ourselves. Because we have defined what we see by using belief and opinion, rather than Truth, we have created an illusion, an unTruth. We are thus blinded from the Truth of our being by these beliefs and opinions; everything we perceive and demonstrate is born out of blindness, ignorance.

What good does seeing one living blindly do for us—or even for the one called blind? If we take this question to our inward Source, the answer we would most likely receive is something like this (although you might better go inward and ask the question for yourself): First of all, whatever parents the way of living in ego consciousness is the ego, which isn't real at all. It's just a figment of our own design. The ego is what we create to justify living from a view that Life is about separation and, therefore, duality. Therefore, ego itself cannot be to blame for the ego conscious viewpoint. Neither can we be held responsible, the ones who maintain ego consciousness as something real. After all, we obtained our views largely from others, both individually and from the collective consciousness. Either way, ego consciousness is akin to a bad dream, which, when we are aware, frees us to live anew. The bad dream felt real while we were dreaming the dream—or having a nightmare—but when we return to our awareness of Christ consciousness, we clearly realize the nightmare was, truly, only a dream, and not at all real. Yet, just like with lucid dreaming, we can shift all the actors and any of their actions, and change the outcome of the dream.

Therefore, from a spiritual perspective, being born blind is not about assigning blame or accusing someone of a sin because of the blindness. Being born blind is only a metaphor for the spiritual ignorance we use to bring order to our lives. To make it as clear as possible, whenever we sense any form of blindness, this is a sure sign that we are falsely trying to order our lives out of ego consciousness, from the foundation of our beliefs and opinions, however determined. Having discerned the error of our ways, we simply part the veil of illusion and restore our lives and our spiritual sight by exercising The Inward Journey.

Having restored our sight—'cured our blindness'—using spiritual or Christ consciousness as our guiding light, we are duty-bound to fulfill each instance of inspirational resonance discerned—each 'aha moment', each element of Truth lighting our way. As long as we maintain our commitment to The Inward Journey, we are enlightened. So, when temporarily blind, we are giving witness to a belief in the reality and power of illusion, giving matter in and of itself power and substance it doesn't have. Illusion and matter have power only because we believe that they do have power and reality. We are to cleanse ourselves of material vision—vision based on the ego conscious perspective—and affirm in its place the spiritual perspective as the form of all substance. When we live from the inside out, all we see is spiritual, divine, and this forms the substance of the spiritual perspective—which is Love, and Love alone. After all is said and done, Life is not for learning—such a declaration only reinforces the ego conscious idea that we need to improve what we are—that we need to know something we already have at our disposal. Life is not about improving anything. Life is about becoming aware of our divinity—simply *remembering* that we *already are* divine—and living true only to this awareness.

Of course, whenever someone shifts perspective from illusion to reality—from ego consciousness to Christ consciousness—others will notice what an amazing difference it has made in the one who now lives out of Christ consciousness. Often, those who notice will ask how this amazing shift has come about, to which the changed one might well respond this way: 'I cleansed my view and demonstration of Life. I now go inward, to the Source of Truth, for my guidance. No longer am I blind. Now I can see. No longer am I deaf. Now I can hear.'

Such a change cannot come about through ego consciousness—which refers only to physicality and not spirituality. Neither can real (spiritual) change come about through some special ritual or a particular medical treatment. Shifts in perspective from material to spiritual are available to anyone, anytime, anywhere, simply by exercising spiritual discernment and returning to the center of their Being, to the sacred Source found by listening inward. Once aware of Truth discerned inward, we comprehend that Truth prophesizes its fulfillment once faithfully committed to.

No matter what the explanation by the one transcended, there will continue to be those who remain skeptical, mostly out of ignorance—lacking experience or understanding of the ways of Christ consciousness. The skeptic, however, normally asks other skeptics or ego conscious persons how this 'cure of blindness' could have occurred. If even modestly spiritually aware, the skeptic would instead defer the answer to any who had transcended through the means of Christ consciousness. Christ consciousness witnessed speaks for itself, after all. Life tells us the skeptic normally continues to search out the reason for the 'cure', the transformation, wanting some external validation with which the skeptic can agree. The search for outer validation of physical law continues, even angrily sometimes—or is the primary stimulus envy?

Somewhere along the search for physical evidence, or magic— either will do for a skeptic—the skeptic will be asked if he/she believes that what comes from God—spiritual Truth—can change one's Life, transcend the perspective from which one lives. Such a query is sure to ignite a spark of enlightenment in the skeptic. When put in this perspective, the new context conveys the obvious Truth—even to the skeptic: the one who has transcended by The Inward Journey is evidence clear enough. Indeed, transcendence—much like Christ consciousness demonstrated— speaks for itself. The glorious witness to Life lived in Christ consciousness provides evidence in ways which ignite inner awareness in others, so they, too, may be enlightened to a new way of living. And the skeptic, now at least partially aware, knows in an instant that he/she can also make the leap.

No longer can the skeptic who comes to hear 'the still, small voice', remain blind to the Truth of the matter, and he comes now to make the Life-changing decision for himself. Should he remain a skeptic, even in the face of Truth, the guilt for having chosen out of fear will be plenty enough for him to handle. It would have been better for him not to know Truth at all.

Chapter Ten

'...they failed to understand what he was saying to them. So
Jesus spoke to them again:
"In all truth I tell you,
I am the gate of the sheepfold.
All who have come before me
are thieves and bandits,
but the sheep took no notice of them.
I am the gate.
Anyone who enters through me will be safe:
such a one will go in and out
and will find pasture."'

From what we've seen so far about living from the inside out, if
one doesn't go inward, they cannot hear the inward voice. It
would be like trying to steal one's way into a movie by walking
into a grocery store. The twain shall never meet. In the case of
The Inward Journey, we hear the still, small voice inspiring us
with endless streams of Wisdom, and they become our own to
demonstrate, one by each, faithfully and fully. As long as we give
our awareness to Wisdom, it feeds us with spiritual
nourishment, the guidance we need for living spiritually from
day to day. Being unaware, however, such wisdom lays fallow in
the fields of ignorance, arrogance and vanity. The 'tin ear' can
never hear perfect pitch, no matter how often perfect pitch is
played or sung.

As we listen to the Truth, we see that all other means of
finding Truth from outward signs have failed us. Again, the voice
speaking inward cannot be heard outwardly; there is only one
Source, one Authority for Life, and Source is not found in the
material world, where so many still search. The one who goes
inward will find a direct passage to Truth, while those who stay

on the outer path think they can find peace in the ego conscious world—as if they could steal what they want where it cannot be found.

When we are spiritually aware, Truth brings fullness to Life. Indeed, Truth lays itself on the line for us, so our lives can be filled with only highest good. Contrarily, ego consciousness feeds on fear and a code of separation, so when we are engaging life from ego consciousness we run away from any Truth seeming counter to the illusions we take for granted, that seem familiar and therefore real to us. Unfortunately, in many cases, those living out of ego consciousness either are offended or scared by any display of Truth. Living in duality, they see the choice as either Truth or ego consciousness. Ignorance engenders those feelings in us, where Christ consciousness instead opens the door only to Wisdom, our Life-long companion. Without question, Truth and awareness of Truth are fully cognizant of one another. Truth breathes Life into awareness—and then into Being, with awareness carrying Truth forward.

There is an endless stream of guidance from the inward Source, and the guidance always leaps into our command as we become aware of its presence in our lives. Inspiration provides the direction, followed by our faithful demonstration of the direction discerned. Although inspiration seems to have disappeared at this point, this is not so. Endlessly, inspiration lies in waiting—and comes alive in us as we become aware yet again. We could easily call this continual flow of loving guidance a 'perpetual motion machine', but to label sacred communication with a mechanistic term is to render Truth or Wisdom a major disservice. Besides, when we strip labels away, we see all is God, Truth, Love, Life, the voice of Wisdom, or Christ consciousness, no matter what else we think it is. Such a rich spiritual perspective presents a dilemma to the ego conscious individual; on one hand he/she thinks that Wisdom comes from some mysterious—and therefore evil—place, while on the other hand he/she sees those who follow The Inward Journey living from a very different and wholesome perspective.

'The Father, for what he has given me, is greater than anyone,
and no one can steal anything from the Father's hand.
The Father and I are one.'

Each day presents an opportunity for us to celebrate a feast, to feast on spiritual Truth. While most think of feasts as a time of consuming great amounts of food and drink, the central theme permeating all spiritual feasts is an inner beckoning that takes us to our spiritual center, our heart of hearts, so we can be still and hear the voice of God—and be nourished by the voice of God and that voice alone. As we walk in the continual presence of Christ consciousness, resisting its Wisdom not one wit, we come to witness the fullness of spiritual Power out into the world. It is then that we can truthfully say, 'He whom hath seen me hath seen my Father'—all who have witnessed my demonstration of inspirational guidance have witnessed the inspiration itself, which gave birth to my demonstration. Indeed, it is awareness that parents inspiration into demonstration.

Those who are unfamiliar, still, with the workings of Christ consciousness—yet who are touched on some level of being by it—often want a direct reference for the Source. Unfortunately, they don't yet have the ears to hear the Source, nor the eyes with which to see the Truth. No matter how those living from Christ consciousness demonstrate its guidance, those unfamiliar with Christ consciousness fail to make the connection between the demonstration and the Source of the demonstration. No matter how many times they are told or are helped to see this ineffable connection, the ineffable connection just doesn't resonate with those embedded in ego consciousness. On the other hand, those living from Christ consciousness are fully aware that there is only one real—spiritual—Source, and it cannot be revealed unless inwardly, nor ever lost. Wisdom and its demonstration always have been, are now, and always will be, One—and thus inseparable.

Still, even as luminously as the numinous glows, there are those who cast aspersions at any who bring Truth into being. Why is this so? Surely, it cannot be that they cast aspersions because of such soulfully rich demonstrations themselves. No, that's not why they cast aspersions. Those under the ego conscious influence feel that to demonstrate Truth is the act of God and not man, so to do so is considered blasphemous to the ways of ego consciousness. Those who cannot see beneath the surface of Life's demonstrations have no clue that the demonstration and its source are One, the same—for they are accustomed to seeing only outer signs, not inward Truth, Wisdom, demonstrated. The spiritual connection simply escapes them.

One day, however, those who live out of ego consciousness will come to see that even if they do not believe the one who demonstrates from his/her center of Christ consciousness, on some level they will at least have an inkling that the real form of goodness comes from a place with which they're not familiar. This awareness will be the beginning of the end, for further down the spiritual path they will also come to see true goodness coming only from the highest Source. Then, they are just a moment's awareness away from seeing the at-one-ment of Source and its demonstration. An extraordinary Light will then have infused them with the deeper meaning and Source of Truth. From this point on, there is no looking back—only unceasing steps on the path of Christ consciousness.

At some point, those formerly of the ego conscious persuasion will see spiritual Truth as the only God we are to worship, and we worship this God by adhering to Truth's guidance for us. When following Truth, we see our demonstrations and our identity becoming One, just as our demonstration and its Source are One—

inseparable. We are our inspirations delivered into the Universe, and cannot be separated from them. Our demonstrations become our identity. Our demonstrations exhibit our character—they *are* our character. Indeed, if I demonstrate out of ego consciousness, I will be identified with those very demonstrations, as will my character. If I commit my life to the principles and acts of greed, gluttony and self-centeredness, I will be identified as greedy, gluttonous and narcissistic by such exhibitions. I will have validated such results as corresponding with ego consciousness, a simply and completely *ordinary* reality—common to all others of like kind.

On the other hand, as I demonstrate out of the leadings of Christ consciousness, I am identified by exhibitions of love, and my character speaks only to loving. Whether we can admit it to ourselves or not, living out of Christ consciousness is to live an *extraordinary* Life in what still, unfortunately, is the very ordinary reality practiced around us. Once aware of this Truth, we arrest our old beliefs and opinions and succumb or surrender to Truth only. Bathed and baptized now in Wisdom, which enlightens, the unbeliever comes full circle to his/her spiritual Home, clothing him/herself only in Christ consciousness from then on. As the extraordinary demonstrates its face, full-flush into the Universe, the ordinary reality fades from view. The theatre lights dim, the curtain parts—and Life begins for real.

Chapter Eleven

'The disciples said, "Rabbi, it is not long since the Jews were trying to stone you; are you going back there again?" Jesus replied:
> "Are there not twelve hours in the day?
> No one who walks in the daytime stumbles,
> having the light of this world to see by;
> anyone who walks around at night stumbles,
> having no light as a guide."'

At one time or another we sense our inner and outer presence lacking congruence. Our penchant for material life has such a strong hold on us that we neglect the more important means of spiritual discernment and demonstration. We feel 'out to sea', 'off balance', 'in this world but not of it'. We feel a gnawing in our gut, sensing something is awry with us. It becomes so strong that we soon feel the need to surrender to something deeper: some mysterious force we instinctively know will pull us out of our misery. Having neglected our highest good ourselves, we feel the need to be saved by someone or something we can trust for this dramatic shift in discernment and purpose—someone or some way of a purer Love rather than the love of things and material attachment. Instinctively, we know material import and ego conscious attachment can serve us no longer.

Neither can looking to outward signs continue to serve us. Looking to outer authority for personal validation and role identification leave us hollow inside, like an egg with no yolk— life without Soul. Indeed, Spirit calls us to be as the innocent child within us, returning to the purity of Spirit to direct us on our path. During this initial discernment, it feels like we are about to die. Indeed, a part of us once thought to be the *only* thing providing our direction in life *is* about to die. It *must* die—for this pattern of living is no longer purposeful and proper for us. To continue in this path of living for the material is to crucify the spiritual Self. And we feel the pain of suffering and death approaching fast upon us—a feeling much like physical death itself.

What we need in such circumstances is a deep and abiding awakening, purposed by a jubilant celebration of The Inward Journey, a calling out of the old ways, so the new means of spiritual discernment can replace them. Then the sudden awareness of Christ consciousness strikes us, calling us Home to our spiritual reality. It is to our innate innocence, the voice of intuition and deeper meaning—Wisdom—we must return. It is from enlightenment that we are transformed, leaping the gap of transcendence to be born anew. Otherwise, we remain in ignorance, and have no light to show the way. We stumble in the darkness of our own making, ignorant of Truth awaiting only awareness—Truth, serving as the beacon to light our way—spiritually.

Before coming to this position of spiritual renewal, essentially we are spiritually asleep. True, from time to time we may follow our intuition—if we even know what intuition is—but for the most part we let our egos drive the bus we ride in and call life. When we go so far as to be embedded in ego consciousness beyond even a modest awareness of our inherent spiritual nature, we are dead to the sacred guidance of inner Wisdom. We instead rest our manifestations in intellect or our own self-importance. We make our ideas, beliefs and opinions the be-all and end-all of our existence. We are the makers of our lives, day-to-day and, 'by golly, no one knows better than I do what's best for me'. Such words describe nothing but the self-important way. We are dead to the possibility and potentiality of spiritual discernment when abiding self-importance. Truly, we are entombed by self-importance.

Contrarily, when we roll away the stone blocking the door to spiritual reality and freedom, we succumb to our more natural state of humility. Humility is a state where we admit we *do not* know what's really best for us, and so we surrender to the still, small voice of Christ consciousness, wisdom, intuition, enlightenment—God by whatever name—as the guiding Light and Power in our lives.

Giving way to Christ consciousness clears away the stone or blockage that formerly kept us blind, rendered us asleep or dead to the inward Truth of our being. As we give more and more credence and commitment to Christ consciousness, we are cleared of more and more of what buried us in the first place. Eventually, yet all at once on the 'healing' continuum, we come to Life; our eyes are opened to The Inward Journey as the path we must tread. The ways of ego consciousness no longer appeal to us, and they fight for their lives and for control of ours. When in this state of inner chaos, we long unabashedly for a better way, for a lifting of what now pains us, and to be caressed by the tender innocence of Spirit. Getting to this stage takes us to the threshold of our own Truth, gaining inner confidence that our resurrection is just around the corner. Belief is not what gets us the rest of the way. It's an inner 'heart knowing' propelling us onward—gnosis, a deep and indelible imprint of Truth on our hearts enlightening our way, even while our habitual commitment to the ways of ego consciousness holds us still in tow, ever so slightly, but in tow, nevertheless. A huge infusion of Love of Self overcomes ego's last gasp, the last attachment to its shallow ways—a Love surging to the surface in such dimensions as to affirm true Love's inherent Power in our lives.

This same Love and spiritual cleansing makes for the blind to see and the deaf to hear. It is a Love unfettered by human constraint or condition—Love so deep and so precious as to be worthy of a holy or sacred relationship—a sacred relationship showing its impeccable nature in a holy instant. It is the Love of Self running so deeply—a Life of adhering and demonstrating

Christ consciousness so completely—as to become a self-fulfilling prophecy. Once fully engaged, Christ consciousness demonstrates from us, *as* us, only, what it is—and what we most naturally are. The voice of Christ consciousness is like a thunderous clap! We can no longer ignore its reality in our Being. We are stuck by lightning, unbound and made free—to live the Truth of our Being.

To be sure, as we traverse this marvelous spiritual journey, there are those who will dispute our way—even our right to engage the way—for to give it credence would be to deny their own way as the correct way. There are those who are so threatened by the potential for enlightenment that they would do anything to avert it. They would go even so far as to gather support from the vast mass of others beholding ego consciousness, to kill off even the deeper idea of spiritual discernment, let alone those who imbibe its long, sweet draught. The strong-willed, bent on destruction of anything or anyone contrary to the ego conscious way, hold their determination to destroy. Determination notwithstanding, the example we set by transcending ego consciousness for Christ consciousness shines the light of Truth on The Inward Journey as 'the Way' for others to traverse, as well. Undeniably, others await the beacon, so as not to stumble from pillar to post out of ignorance. Holding steadfast to the beacon of Truth casts enlightenment far and wide, shedding fear's illusions in every corner of its wake. And those who see and follow the light come to land safely in the harbor of Truth.

Chapter Twelve

'So Jesus said, "Leave her alone; let her keep it (the ointment) for the day of my burial. You have the poor with you always, you will not always have me."'

As we transcend our spiritual path from ego consciousness to our more authentic way of Being, we are reminded of the ways of old along the way. We are tempted to return our focus on material life and spiritualizing the ego, making material attachment look real to the uninitiated, when material attachment is not real at all. Attachment is not real because it is we who attach ourselves to the material; there is no inherent attachment that can be attributed to material life itself. In and of itself, attachment is an attitude or belief we use as our lenses for viewing a particular situation or circumstance. What is real is tending to our spiritual focus, looking inward—applying the sacred ointment of Truth to every step we take along the way.

There will be those among us who will think us wrong, that we should commit ourselves to a dualistic unreality without reserve, using our energy for spiritualizing and validating ego conscious-ness as the guidance we ought to obey. For the time being, at least, the all too common way of ego consciousness will be the one most frequently observed around us. Obviously, there is a mix of those who know the Truth exhibited by The Inward Journey and those who hate it out of difference from their own way. Without question, the hate strikes out not only at the Journey, but also at those who prove the journey's worth by its very existence and example.

'...this was another reason why the crowd came out to receive him: they had heard he had given this sign. Then the Pharisees said to one another, "You see, you are making no progress; look, the whole world has gone after him!"'

When we become comfortable wearing our 'new clothes', the garments of inner peace garnered through increased spiritual poise and confidence, we attract others of similar interest to the fore. A strong inner core of spirituality provides a clear sign that we are in the final stages of crucifying personality, and are fast approaching the fullness of living in Christ consciousness. Others want to join us, which is all the more reason for us to maintain our primary seat in the lap of humility: knowing no Truth but the Wisdom discerned through Christ consciousness.

At first, it's only natural for those who wish for a similar spiritual journey to feel confused or be put off by the necessity of remaining humble. Such a major shift in one's journey is commanding and seems complex, sometimes even unruly. Yet, when followers commit more fully to transcending the old for the new, the value of humility returns quickly to view. Keeping witness to The Inward Journey draws even more to the richly loving example.

The prospect of rising numbers of supporters for the spiritual example can often enrage those still unwilling to honor even a semblance of the spiritually loving example as important to their own lives. After all, to honor something contrary to their beliefs would be to betray their religious heritage. It is in this juxtaposition between living spiritually and abiding external law and form where the meaning of religion is redefined. While being religious is akin to obeying written law by those of the ego conscious persuasion, for those of Christ consciousness, religion comes to take on the meaning of whatever it is we use to give spiritual order to our lives from day to day.

Either out of ego consciousness or Christ consciousness, what we demonstrate from moment to moment is what we practice religiously. To what is demonstrated using ego consciousness as the daily guide we call the reflections of self-importance—some religious practice or belief, which says ego consciousness can overpower Truth and rule the day. To what is demonstrated from the foundation of Christ consciousness we assign the simple term humility: a deep inner knowing in our heart of hearts—gnosis, heart knowing—which says Truth can demonstrate only what it is and not some erroneous belief or opinion—but a mere facsimile of Truth. Spiritually, then, religious practice is about freeing the power of Christ consciousness into the Universe, so others may also be guided and enlightened by its golden glow. So they, too, are inspired to have their lives ordered in a much deeper and more purposeful manner.

> 'Jesus replied to them:
> ..."In all truth I tell you,
> unless a wheat grain falls into the earth and dies,
> it remains only a single grain;
> but if it dies
> it yields a rich harvest.
> Anyone who loves his life loses it;
> anyone who hates his life in this world
> will keep it safe for eternal life."'

Wishing to find a better life, converts of all sorts are attracted to The Inward Journey. In such times, the voice of Christ consciousness is glorified by the exponential increase in spiritual discernment by those new to the fold. Unless the old ways give way completely to the new, however, the new will lay fallow. Lacking enlightenment, ignorance maintains the rule of the day. If the old ways are allowed to truly die, the new can take root and eventually bloom into being. Anyone who clings assiduously to a life in ego consciousness loses the larger view of spiritual guidance, seemingly forever. Whoever follows the voice of Christ consciousness becomes at one with Christ consciousness, and is served by its Truth—is in fact honored and glorified by the Truth as it comes into daily demonstration. Should those serving as the living example of Christ consciousness draw back from their inherent charge to lead by example? Hardly! In the deepest folds of spiritual awareness, this very purpose of example is what commits to Christ consciousness in the first place.

When we glorify Christ consciousness by our demonstration—our example—it is as though a voice rings out from the heavenly realms, declaring its Truth to the world. Example touches others deeply, much like a bump in the night sets us free from worry and fret. To be validated this way is an honor, to be sure. This spiritually pure voice sounds out to the Universe, as in all of us, announcing a commanding presence of spiritual power, which can and will dislodge others from the miasma of fear, drawing them instead to the bosom of inner peace and joy.

Getting a glimpse of enlightenment gives impetus for transcending ignorance, darkness. Once touched, we move forward to enlightenment with dispatch, lest we return unwittingly to our past. It is only through an unrelenting investment in the timeless gifts of intuition that we become children of enlightenment—in the perfect image and likeness thereof. Not in the same form, perhaps, but in the image and likeness just the same—the essence of spiritual reality: divinity.

'Indeed, they were unable to believe... And yet there were many who did believe in him, even among the leading men... Jesus declared publicly:
"Whoever believes in me
believes not in me
but in the one who sent me,
and whoever sees me,
sees the one who sent me.
I have come into the world as light,
to prevent anyone who believes in me
from staying in the dark anymore."'

Even though the disenchanted may, from time to time, see the many extraordinary outer signs associated with Christ consciousness, many—perhaps even most—still cannot allow themselves to see anew. The ways of ego consciousness have blinded them, rendered them dead to the marvelous potential and reality of living spiritually. To the uninformed and fear-filled, changing their ways is most improbable. They put personal glory before the glory of Christ consciousness, betraying themselves before the eyes of the heavens. Fearing being banned by the likes of their own kind, spiritually they shrivel and eventually die from lack of spiritual nourishment.

The Truth about Christ consciousness says that whatever we see as the demonstration of its sacredness speaks to us on a level deeper than simple appearance. When truly discerned, the value of spiritual appearance penetrates to the core of our spiritual being—its resonance indicates to us the one true Source, unmistakably so. This is the purpose of Christ consciousness: to enlighten us as we give ourselves to inward discernment.

Anyone who fails to see the value of The Inward Journey comes to judge himself, because, at the deepest level of being, even the uninformed and unbelieving know there is a better way, their unawareness, beliefs and opinions notwithstanding. Perhaps one day they will see, just like those who abide Christ consciousness do, that living from a foundation of Christ consciousness is an eternal affair—a relation with Truth and its demonstration which ignites the heart with the infinitude of Truth's guidance.

Chapter Thirteen

'In all truth I tell you,
whoever welcomes the one I send, welcomes me,
and whoever welcomes me, welcomes the one who sent me.'

As we move forward with our spiritual transformation, we come to think we need to change what we are into something we'd like better—the fullness of our divinity.

However, in its purest sense, spirituality is about transcending, not transforming. If we think we need to change something, the need for change is a sure sign that we're standing in ego consciousness, both feet planted. Transcendence deals with 'leapfrogging' the erroneous idea of needing to fix or change ourselves, and instead surrendering to the Truth of the matter. Spiritually speaking, nothing needs fixing or changing. Spiritually speaking, there's only one thing we *can* be: divine. God is All That Is—and God is divine and perfect. So, too, are we simply divine—and just perfect, thank you!

When we get the idea that we need to cleanse the spiritual foundation supporting our very being, we can be sure it's ego consciousness calling us to the task. Should we find ourselves there, in ego consciousness, a few questions we might ask to good advantage are: What's to fix? Who's doing the fixing? And who or what is it that's being fixed? Whenever we find ourselves asking about some 'who' or 'why', we can be sure that we're in ego consciousness. Such a calling is the call of dualistic thought and needs no attention paid to it whatsoever.

Instead, if we would just remember to go inward, we would find Christ consciousness affirming our divinity, and would behave exactly that way: divinely. We would live our divinity through *all* we demonstrate—and duality would thus cease to exist. This is the only 'cleansing' that need occur—we call it simply, 'awareness' — and it's not nearly the same as that required by ego consciousness. A major shift occurs in us when we finally realize that cleansing has nothing to do with changing us. We simply need to *remember* what we really *already* are — always have been, and always will be. It's *remembrance* that really does the trick, you see. When we re-member ourselves with the Truth of what we are, we are One. If we surrender to this Truth about us — that we are God, inseparable and thus divine — then we stabilize our spiritual reality *as* divine. Taking any other perspective or path returns us to the only thing it can: the illusion created by a dualistic way of thinking, found only in the erroneous idea of ego consciousness.

Demonstrating spiritual transcendence allows us to be the example of remembrance for others. Our spiritual purpose has nothing to do with fixing or changing others — helping them shift from ego consciousness to spiritual or Christ consciousness. Our spiritual purpose is only to remind others — simply by the example we set — that there is only *one* existence, not *two*. There is not God *and* something else, something opposed to God. There is only God. God is All That Is. If God is All That Is, we too are All That Is, God, and therefore we need no changing at all. All we need to do is remember that we are God — and Godliness is the Truth about us. When we do remember — re-member with the God we are — we automatically behave true to our Godliness. Our Word — our calling and demonstration — are at One, inseparable. Surely, then, we understand that the example of re-membrance is the one we cast out into the world. As we cast this Truth out into the ethers, we can be sure we who convey it, and the message itself, also are One.

Therefore, it would be a mistake of major proportions for us to think that 'washing someone's feet' — or our own — is our purpose. Washing our feet is not about cleansing our spiritual foundation by undoing the multifarious ego conscious imagery we falsely take to be the Truth about us. Likewise, it would be a mistake to think that being humble means we ought to serve others by cleansing them of their erroneous ways. Such an expression of humility would serve only to reinforce the idea of something in another needing to be changed or fixed. How could it be that God—the God each is—needs to be changed or fixed? From a spiritual perspective, this would be tantamount to blasphemy. God—we—are perfect just as we are. Should we forget this, however, the untoward result is not far away.

Whenever we dine at the table of at-One-ment—welcoming this gift of Truth about us—we honor the gift, the inspiration of remembrance that took us there in the first place. Should we fail to recognize the gift that remembrance brings to us, and instead dine on the illusions of dualistic ego consciousness, we obviate the opportunity to bring glory only to Truth. The sure sign of our spiritual integrity shows itself in the choices we make about what it is we abide, take in, as the Truth we are to demonstrate. We glorify Truth only as we walk *in* Truth, just as we glorify and express our gratitude for a gift of a sweater, for example, not only with our words, but by actually *wearing* the sweater. In both cases, the Truth found in demonstration both validates and celebrates Truth. In the end, we actually wear the Truth as our identity, while at the same time express our gratitude.

In the same way, we are giving gratitude for inspiration by being only what we are. Words can never convey gratitude, for, spiritually speaking, our supreme gratitude is demonstrated only by living what we truly are. As we occupy our innocence, we come to know that there is no outer authority we can justifiably follow. Likewise, just as some outer authority leaves our presence, we come to know this or any other outer authority cannot really serve as Truth to or for us.

When we come to live by this principle, the principle of at-One-ment, we see all as divine, and honor all precisely *as* divine. This example is the perfect personification of loving our neighbor as ourselves, and will identify each of us as disciples of

The Inward Journey. Truly, we cannot know where Truth goes or comes from until we learn we are Truth lived. Then we know there is nothing but Truth to be lived. When we set about thinking that we have given up our lives for Truth—have somehow committed to changing ourselves so we can become divine—we cement ourselves further in ego consciousness. In order to be set free, in order to be complete, we need only return to the remembrance that we already *are* divine, *are* God and thus are *already* complete. We then penetrate our ego conscious chrysalis and flutter out into the Universe in all our magnificence—much like the Monarch butterfly reminds us of the beauty of our true image and likeness, setting us free at last.

Chapter Fourteen

'I shall ask the Father,
and he will give you another Paraclete
to be with your forever,
the Spirit of truth
whom the world can never accept
since it neither sees nor knows him;
but you know him,
because he is with you, he is in you.'

Often, these days, we seem to walk around with troubled hearts. True, whenever we take ourselves to the troubles of the world, well, there we are—troubled. Should we put our thoughts and minds there, troubles grow into larger troubles, occupying us more and more. Tension builds, uneasiness grows, and our dissatisfaction with life as we know it does the same.

On the other hand, when we focus inward—no matter what circumstances we meet throughout the day—we will have placed our faith in something far more rewarding: our inherent peace of mind and joy-filled heart. Indeed, there are many perspectives available to take us beyond worry and fret, angst and concern. Our Kingdom is not of this realm, but found inward. It seems as though the Serenity Prayer used in Alcoholics Anonymous fits perfectly here: 'God grant me the serenity to accept the things I cannot change, the courage to change the things I can and the wisdom to know the difference.'

We cannot change the machinations of the planet, but we can change how we see the planet, and behave accordingly. When we slow down enough to touch Truth inward, we find our innate, unlimited capacity for 'knowing the difference' awaiting our awareness, and our re-membrance. Once aware, we find this to be the only place where we find peace and joy. Never can peace and joy be found elsewhere. While it may look like we have come to peace and joy outwardly, the appearance of such is short-lived—simply because appearance is a figment of our imagination, and not the Truth of the matter. In fact, and in Truth, we *are* peace and joy, just waiting to be expressed.

When abiding inwardly, we are automatically taken to Truth—mainly because the inward Source *is* Truth. When we or another of us questions the nature or location of Truth, all we need do is remember that The Inward Journey is the only path to the Truth that breathes Life into being. No one can find Truth where Truth cannot be found—outward. By the same token, when we come to recognize and abide Truth, at the same time we are honoring the Source of that Truth—the inspiration that brings enlightenment into being. We all recognize intuition's calling when we hear it—and we all know this calling is the only real one to follow.

There are those around us who look only outward for direction, for the signs they think speak Truth to them. The best outer signs can do is point us back to the inward Source. Our heart resonates only with Truth, yet, often, we follow Truth not. Upon reflection, we see our heart's content settled only inwardly, yet much of the time we behave as though this were not so. Forgetfulness is strong, and operates often, leaving us in a stupor, following essentially one empty dream after another.

As we follow The Inward Journey, others will come to ask how it is that we appear so happy. How is it that we seem to know our purpose? How is it that we seem free to be what we are called to be? Such questions form out of a misplaced sense of spiritual reality. They see happiness and joy, a fulfilled sense of purpose and celebration of freedom, and they think we have somehow caused them to be. If only they would look inward, they would find the *real* cause: Truth, Wisdom, speaks freely from them, as well—if only they would give Truth and Wisdom credence their awareness. Once connected with Truth, Truth is what must speak, which provides the freedom to just Be. From this point on, Truth, Wisdom, speaks for itself. We need not give ourselves to making Truth come to Life. The works showing themselves outward are thus the proverbial 'proof of the pudding', and neither the cause nor the effect. The works serve only to validate inspiration as awareness demonstrated.

Once The Inward Journey is discerned and abided, we find our works abounding, not because we are making them happen—manifesting them—but because our awareness has opened the door for each inspiration to come into Life, simply by honoring the gifts, each in our own way. And gratitude meets enlightenment on the road to fulfillment. Whenever we become aware of what we are inspired to demonstrate, and acknowledge it with loving intention, this very thing will become the evidence of the commandment put into being. Each demonstration glorifies the image that gives it Life—which fathers or parents it into Being in the first place.

Those of us who give credence to The Inward Journey know Spirit propels Wisdom forward, and follow only this path. Quite quickly, we come to adhere only to Truth, and forget that there was any other way. We come thus to equate Love with this journey; comprehending loving oneself is to tread this path only. We Love our neighbors likewise, giving them only what we find inward, and emboldening them to travel in Love's way, as well. From then on, we give ourselves totally to loving and demonstrating the fullness of Love conveyed, and nothing less. This commitment opens the door to the unlimited, fathomless Source, having no end.

Anyone who sees The Inward Journey with spiritual eyes will come also to keep the Word, and demonstrate the images of Truth, of Wisdom, whole and complete. This is the promise of the Law of Order, and it speaks only to what is whole and complete when spiritually discerned. The voice of Wisdom enlightens us to all we need know, just for giving ourselves to awareness of its presence in our lives. And each time we come to awareness, we are reminded yet again of its Power in our lives as the only source of love and peace and joy we are honor bound to be, to live, and to give, wrapped in peace of mind and joy-filled heart—Love personified. We know in this instant that we are Home to stay—indeed, we are Home itself.

Chapter Fifteen

'You are clean already,
by means of the word I have spoken to you.
Remain in me, as I in you.
As a branch cannot bear fruit all by itself,
unless it remains part of the vine,
neither can you unless you remain in me.'

It also will do us good to remember that any divine inspiration we fail to take to completion will be laid to rest in the field of misperception. It is a major mistranslation of life to leave inspiration's purpose unattended and unfulfilled. Delivering each inspiration to completion is our purpose, and when we maintain Love's intention, each does reach fulfillment. On the other hand, those to which we give no nourishment and intention die of their own accord. When we have distanced ourselves in any way from our divine purpose, we fail to hear Wisdom awaiting our awareness. How, then, can we bear the fruit each gift has in store? Like the baby lamb leaving its mother out of curiosity or distraction, the milk lays fallow in the mother's breast. Yet, without attending to the breast, the lamb is not fed, and thus cannot have a full and prosperous Life. We are no different when we become distracted. When we leave the milk of inspiration unattended—our spiritual nourishment—we cannot have a full and prosperous Life.

When we remain connected with our only real Source, we bear fruit aplenty. Without this inner connection, we can do nothing spiritual in nature—which is our only true nature. Thus, we become disenchanted, in disarray and unfilled, lacking purpose. Using these feelings to guide us back home—to the one and only Source—inspiration frees us to demonstrate our spiritual nature again and again, just because we showed up and listened. When we hear this glorious voice of inspiration yet again—and take the first step toward completion—each succeeding step is made aware, precisely as we are guided to listen inwardly, precisely as and when each step is needed. Life cannot be simpler than this—nor more rewarding and fulfilling than this. Thus is prayer defined—and fulfilled: to show up and listen, and then to demonstrate inspiration discerned.

Following this example is precisely the example we provide for others. As we are given, so is inspiration delivered unto others. We—and all who are further inspired to live by the example they see lived by us—come to live the real definition of Love: to be what we are called to Be. By adhering to this inner calling, and none other, we are fulfilling the commandment of Love's way, The Inward Journey. We become inspiration's disciples, expanding its power by opening the door to awareness for others by our example. Doing so, we demonstrate Love as we have *been* Loved, giving Truth to one and all. What could be simpler—and more the Truth?

Living in our natural state of spiritual being, we may tend to think we have abandoned choice or free will; we have no individual identity, and all we'd be doing is living an impersonal existence. The term 'personal' is a term embedded in ego consciousness, so its dualistic counterpart—impersonal—can also exist, and keep us in the never-ending battle to maintain one over the other. This is duality at its worst. Knowing we are divine and the only One, how could our identity be clearer and more complete than this? Being *All That Is* lacks nothing, is always fulfilled, and meets Its one and only purpose: to Be. Let's come to the Truth of this with indelible clarity: Being is eternal, immortal and complete, in and of itSelf. Being has only one purpose: demonstrating completeness—inspiration fulfilled. Demonstrating completeness is the only true form of Loving, for it brings to the Universe the Truth of our Being and nothing less, nothing inauthentic—only unadorned, unmasked Truth fulfilled—this and this alone.

'If you belonged to the world,
the world would love you as its own;
but because you do not belong to the world,
because my choice of you has drawn you out of the world,
that is why the world hates you.'

Should you decide to live anew, demonstrating only what you really are into the Universe—divine—there are many who will envy and dislike you. Don't take it personally. Easy for me to say, I know; yet, if others display envy or dislike—perhaps even disdain what they think you're doing and who they falsely think you are—these responses are only because they don't yet comprehend what living spiritually means. Their particular view doesn't make them bad; it only means they're not yet aware or may have forgotten—and are thus only different from what we are. Not worse, nor not as good—just different. Unfortunately, mere difference puts some people off. You have dared to step out of a commitment to ego consciousness into another way, The Inward Journey, and walk only on this path. Indeed, this does make you different—but not better or worse, as some would think.

When you are being judged, others' treatment of you is about 'shooting the messenger', rather than about 'hearing the message'. As yet, they cannot hear the message, so they focus on you, the messenger—the deliverer of another way, of bringing Truth out into the open. Not so unusual, is it? Don't we—at the very least—become confused when confronted by a completely new way of looking at something or someone? Or course we do! The amazing thing, however, is if we just stand strong in the example we're demonstrating—walking in our Truth—others will get message. Getting the message may take some time, but holding to Truth always delivers what it set out to do. On some level, in some way, it strikes a chord, a chord resonating distinctively as the Truth it is. Perhaps someone will be put on notice that they are to change direction for their life completely. Perhaps this resonance, depending on how deeply it strikes home, will ignite only a simple awareness of 'something is different here'. Or perhaps it will make only a dent in the surface. Each is a treasure, even the dent in the surface, because when enough dents accumulate, they finally tip the table of time and understanding — spreading the disparate elements of ego consciousness onto the floor of disrepair. We thus come to see them for what they are: nothing but empty promises, which cannot ever be fulfilled. And a new dawn begins.

Besides, how another responds to you, or thinks of you, is none of your business. Our only business is to Be. To Be — period.

Had you never showed up in others' lives, being the Loving example you are, others who have yet to understand might well maintain their ignorance, stay buried in their blankets of disillusionment, be dead to the world of Spirit — of Wisdom, of Truth. Because The Inward Journey, in all its simplicity, is unfamiliar still to them, they may well have a visceral reaction rather than a Loving response. Not having the tools to comprehend what they are witnessing, they react, coming to what they see out of reason or reaction rather than Truth. How could this be otherwise, when no one has taught them how to really see and really hear? You are the one to teach this new form of seeing and hearing to them. You are the one who has responded to the inner voice — and all will be better for it. Undoubtedly, by Being what inspiration calls us to Be, we are fulfilling the call. This is teaching simplified — our example does the teaching. We need not work at it, at all.

By demonstrating each intimate step of inspiration along the journey, we *become* the journey. The journey, then — and not we individually — is what witnesses to the Truth or Wisdom lived. This is not to dispel the clarity of our commitment to faithfully follow our calling with all we are, with all our heart and the fullness of Love's intent, for this also witnesses to living spiritually. We thus *are* One, and will be witnessed and lived this way.

There is no turning back now. There is only each 'now' to be lived—passionately, completely and lovingly. Others will join, of this we can be sure—as sure as sure can Be.

Chapter Sixteen

'Still, I am telling you the truth:
it is for your own good that I am going,
because unless I go,
the Paraclete will not come to you;
but if I go,
I will send him to you.
...when the Spirit of truth comes
he will lead you to the complete truth,
since he will not be speaking of his own accord,
but will say only what he has been told;
and he will reveal to you the things to come.'

When we join with inward Truth, others will be confused by the way we have chosen. Not understanding it, they worship other views: those they think will provide them with what they wish for. This disparity will continue to grow, and with it the desire to eliminate The Inward Journey as a legitimate means of living faithfully. For those who differ with The Inward Journey, they will feel the need to excise it from their surroundings, lest it continue to trouble them. We need to know this so we aren't taken by surprise, aren't threatened by the normal response to what is thought to be different—especially when someone is threatened with a lifestyle and way of spiritual knowing so vastly different from their own.

With this being said, from time to time we must reinforce the necessity for being led away from outer authority—even Jesus or Buddha—or we will never go inward to the One and only. Many of us develop unhealthy co-dependencies with others, where we depend on them for answers of all kinds and they depend on us to depend on them. So, often times, unless the one we have depended on pulls away from us, many of us will not come to understand the higher or deeper calling to be heard within *us*. We'll stay reliant on outer authority until we *must*, out of necessity, go *inward* to the only real Source of Truth, of Wisdom, for us.

To miss the essential ingredient of spiritual living—going inward to obtain what we already have available to us for guiding our lives—is to miss the opportunity of a lifetime. To miss this opportunity is to embed ourselves in layer after layer of erroneous information—appropriate for those who share such with us, perhaps—but not at all suitable as spiritual direction for us. After all, we already have all we need for living spiritually, by going inward and listening, while Truth makes us aware. To have engaged with Life otherwise is to have missed the target of how to live spiritually.

Some would say that to miss this target of living spiritually is to define sin. Rest assured that this is not a sin but only a simple mistake—of not living spiritually. A mistake is neither irreversible nor necessitates punishment. A mistake is simply is what it is. See mistake as a sign to change direction—to live spiritually—and begin anew. Thus are guilt and shame rendered nonexistent.

By this awareness, what formerly may have seemed to be treasures to us become clear measures of ego consciousness only. As we shift our focus inward, at some point we suddenly feel flooded with a new sense of freedom—freedom to know and serve only Truth, highest good for us and all around us. Just as suddenly, we come to realize that all we need for each single succeeding step follows. By taking the first step on a new journey, we get to listen for the next—and each succeeding next, one at a time—until what we have been inspired to put into motion has been completely fulfilled. In this fashion, we come to see each of those steps necessary for fulfillment as the complete Truth for us, provided simply by staying aware and faithfully activating their presence.

Just as suddenly as we come into enlightenment, we fully comprehend Truth flowing through all of us in this same way, for Truth is all there really is. When we come to live only Truth, we live in complete harmony, not only with what is right for us, but as One. We transcend the illusion of ego consciousness to become instruments in Life's orchestra, trumpeting only Truth, Being Life's music called into harmony.

'So it is with you; you are sad now,
but I shall see you again, and your hearts will be full of joy,
and that joy no one can take from you.
When that day comes,
you will not ask me any questions.'

For a short time after we break away from outer authority, we feel lost, out to sea, without direction for how to reach safe harbor. Yet, when we go inward with devotion, we find the voice of Truth we thought we heard from outer source coming to us with indelible clarity. Formerly, we heard Truth *through* someone else, a trusted voice—not just anyone—but now we see Truth returned to us without filter of any kind, all for the price of silencing our own beliefs and opinions, so we can hear the Truth spoken within ourselves.

Further, while it may appear that we need to stay 'joined at the hip' with Spirit, once we see how Spirit works—Truth be known and then demonstrated; the next Truth be known and then demonstrated, etc.—we see that it is we who come and go. Truth is always faithfully present, just waiting for us to show up—also faithfully—so we can take a next bite-size piece and then move on to the next, and the next. The Truth seems to disappear from moment to moment when, in fact, it is we who depart the scene from moment to moment. Living spiritually is precisely this way.

Many of us are dismayed at the seeming lack of consistent guidance, until we come to understand that we must invest ourselves completely—the fullness of our commitment and intent and power, not 98% but 100%—in only this journey. Then the journey and we become One. Even further, we come to see it is the journey we are that fulfills, and not some product or outcome that we witness at the end of a particular tributary upon which we've been floating. It would be sad to have left this realm without having sung our song; it would be sadder still to have left this realm without having *lived* our song. And sadder still to have left this realm without coming to Be our song. The song, of course, is the journey we are living—the journey we *are*—lived to the Truth of the journey only. The idea of savoring thus arrives at our doorstep.

Arriving at the base of our song, we also come to see that we need not be at all concerned about our desire to go to a former outer authority for answers. All we need to fulfill our purpose resides within what we already are—and thus have. We need but go inward to discern Truth for us, and demonstrate only Wisdom out into the world at large. In no time at all, we come to discern that there is nothing between the Truth and us, except when we don't show up and really listen. In the final analysis, then, we come to see Truth flowing freely to those who devote themselves only to Truth, simply because they—we—haven't split ourselves between spiritual consciousness and ego consciousness. There's nothing so disconcerting to our spiritual fulfillment than being 98% in spiritual reality. Being part way—even so close as 98%—is hell on Earth, because when we think we are as close as 98% 'there', we then invest our energy in trying to be complete, instead of relaxing into our completeness. As long as we are split, even to this small degree, we erroneously think that we are not fully Home, complete, One. Home is being 100% of what we truly are, and then abiding only that—savoring our Truth, our spiritual reality. In reality, whether we think so or not, we are complete, whole, 100% divine. Period. Nothing else matters.

When in transition from our investment in ego consciousness

to Christ or spiritual consciousness, we will sometimes seem scattered, confused, befuddled by our house divided. The fact remains, however, in the inner Kingdom, Truth is always present, so all we need to reinstate ourselves in Truth's presence is to show up on its doorstep, and we'll sense the door opening so we may indeed enter once again. Finally, we will see the only way to peace is found in demonstrating The Inward Journey. Abiding inward, and inward alone, we conquer all other earthly realms, especially the realm of ego consciousness, for it is inward where we see ego consciousness as no-thing-ness. At last, we come to roost in the Kingdom, which is not of this earth but of Spirit. Home, Home at last.

Chapter Seventeen

'I have revealed your name
to those whom you took from the world to give me.
They were yours and you gave them to me,
and they have kept your word.
Now at last they have recognized
that all you have given me comes from you
for I have given them
the teaching you gave to me,
and they have indeed accepted it
and know for certain that I came from you.'

When we raise our eyes so we can perceive Life spiritually, we feel like a sixth sense has taken over our lives. No longer do we pay attention to outer influences in our day-to-day activities, circumstances and relations. No longer do we feel we're alone, for we sense our lives on a very different level, in a very different way—from the inside, out. It's like someone is sending messages from a secret storehouse of 'rightness' for us, and we hesitate not one moment to judge whether it is right or not. We just *know* it is right for us—and thus for all around us.

Spiritually, in this simple yet profound moment of Truth, glory is brought to both the message and the messenger, for the messenger is but the image and likeness of the message.

What other purpose are we to serve? Revealing Truth and the journey as One completes the example we are here to set. Each of us, by abiding Wisdom, Truth heard inwardly provides the perfect example for living spiritually. Others who also are aware, see and replicate this stunningly beautiful example, for it also resonates with them as Truth, and propels them forward on their own journey. Knowing Truth requires neither translation nor judgment; each who surrenders to The Inward Journey knows with certainty that there is no other legitimate way to live, no other means for living spiritually. We teach best by example, with personal experience validating both the means and the ends. In the case of True Love, the means validate the ends, for Love begets only Love.

Although there are those who would categorize prayer as making petition to some external god, some false idol, The Inward Journey reflects a much different definition of prayer. Prayer along The Inward Journey consists of listening only, listening for the Word of Truth; Truth, which awaits only our unfettered attention and focus, being fully aware. By committing ourselves to spiritual awareness, each of us thus commits also to validating the Truth once heard by demonstrating the Truth heard into being. Thus, prayer is made whole. Prayer defined this way is *always* fulfilled.

Once reflected onto the earth plane, we come to see the demonstration of Truth putting others off in their view of us. Upsetting the apple cart of comfort and material indulgence makes some people very uncomfortable, at the very least, and even antagonizes still others to the point of distraction. Most don't like to see dramatic change, especially if it is unfamiliar to their way of life. It makes them feel like they're wrong, or leaves them feeling less than the ones living from a center of Truth, Wisdom. After all, being 'less than' or 'not good enough' is what most are taught, so most don't know any better. The real diffi-culty, however, rears its head for those who *do* know better and do nothing to change their own dysfunctional pattern.

Still, there is nothing we need do, except continue to live the spiritual example defined as The Inward Journey, for it and it alone depicts living an extraordinary life in what can only be termed an ordinary reality. The outer reality is ordinary because it *is* the norm, the commonly held way in which most people on this planet, in this place of limited spiritual awareness, demon-strate their lives still. The inner reality is extraordinarily simply because it resembles not one iota of what it is not, and instead establishes living spiritually as its only way, without outer distraction of any kind or place.

Much like a beacon shining brightly from a lighthouse on the seashore, we are only to serve as a torch to light the inner fire of Truth. What others do with a sense of impending spiritual awareness is none of our business. Should they turn away from the Truth, even though aware of it, that is none of our business. Should they turn their lives in the direction of Light, even though this would be a good thing from a spiritual perspective, taking responsibility for their action is, likewise, none of our business.

By providing the living example of Unity, others have the opportunity to see Truth, Wisdom, as the foundation for living spiritually. Living from this foundation is the real definition of Love. Without reserve, the spiritual foundation *is* Love itself. As unusual as this declaration of Love may sound to many people, the power of the declaration gives credence and authenticity to the gifts of Love that we offer this way to one and all. Should others come to this same spiritual awareness, they too will be the beneficiaries of Love's true Power in their lives. And so it is—and will be—just as Love always has been.

Chapter Eighteen

'Jesus replied, "Mine is not a kingdom of this world; if my kingdom were of this world, my men would have fought to prevent my being surrendered to the Jews. As it is, my kingdom does not belong here... I was born for this, I came into the world for this, to bear witness to the truth; and all who are on the side of truth listen to my voice."'

As we move through the muddy waters of confused thought, harboring still at least some ego consciousness, we tend to think the muddy waters will take us over. Indeed, it feels like our shift to Christ consciousness is being taken over by darkness in a single moment. The discomfort grows in the shadow of combative thought, all the religious thoughts and priestly authority found in the letter of religious law. Interestingly, when confronted with the Truth of our being, these fade from view. True, it may take more than a single confrontation with these old ideas and beliefs, but in the end Truth is known and the sense of discomfort leaves in Truth's wake. Once we reconnect with inner Wisdom, we realize Wisdom has never left us, only that we have temporarily misplaced or forgotten it. During transitions of this magnitude, particularly from ego to spiritual consciousness, this discomforting 'spasm', as it were, visits us. Fear not. Relaxing the tension around the spasm allows us to re-member with Truth, setting us at ease once again.

When captured by formal religious thought—intellect given to rites and ceremonies and the letter of the Word—without the inner spiritual Truth—the outer attempts to snuff out the inner and all who adhere to the Truth found there. Those who abide the outer cannot fathom the nature and purpose of intuition and inspiration, and the nonresistance of the inner Self to Truth. In their unfamiliarity and discomfort, those embedded in ego consciousness set out to destroy those who demonstrate the example of Truth lived, at least in their own minds.

Interestingly, and sadly, those who are not yet fully adhering to the path of Truth often deny any alliance with it at all. This is not to condemn such persons, only to let you know they exist. Even if we seem fully committed, from time to time we ourselves may 'fall off the wagon', occasionally denying our reliance on Truth as our journey. Again, this is not to condemn, only to point out that it can happen—and to be aware that all it takes to renew one's full commitment is to acknowledge the separation and then return to Unity.

Along The Inward Journey we will be asked by some— usually those who consider themselves separate from inward alliance—what it is we live by. A simple answer is to declare, 'My Life speaks for itself. Merely watch what it is I teach by example.' Discernment need be no more complex than this. Yet, those not allied with spiritual consciousness fear being taken over by spiritual consciousness, and are threatened by it. Once it is understood that spiritual consciousness has nothing to do with material or ego consciousness—and is therefore not in competition with ego consciousness, after all—those who normally fear spiritual consciousness can see it as less than a threat to their way of life. Most then dismiss the supposed threat as nothing at all, and go on their way, mostly ignorant of, and out of touch with, spiritual or Christ consciousness.

So, while others may initially perceive those who fully embrace the Life of Spirit as a threat to them, we can help alleviate their concern by declaring that following our spiritual journey is not an imposition on ego consciousness at all. Our commitment is different, to be sure, but it is not in competition with ego consciousness. Competition is a tool of ego consciousness, not spiritual consciousness. When in spiritual consciousness, we know there is only One, not two, and thus nothing with which to compete. Still, there are those who would hold us guilty of some kind of heresy and wish us to be jailed or silenced. Ironically, it is those very ones who would have jailed themselves in ego consciousness, and thus silenced Truth from Being.

Chapter Nineteen

'You have no power over me at all if it had not been given you from above.'

When the fair-minded turn over their inherent connection with inward Truth to those who abide only ego consciousness, harsh judgments often result. Insults, aspersions, demeaning commentary—all these and more—may at first appear harsher than they really are. However, when walking the journey of our Truth only, we stand tall, understanding that all such judgments and forms of harshness are none of our business, so we pay no attention to them whatsoever. What really matters is staying on course, talking and walking in Wisdom only. We give no power to untruth; only to the Truth we know in our hearts has highest good as its—and our—real purpose. Ego consciousness thus has no power over us, except if we were to abandon our allegiance to Truth.

No doubt, some of those who remain most disconnected from Truth heard inward will feel threatened by one who abides only Truth, so will want to dispel them from their presence. They push such a Truth-abiding person from view, without concern for their welfare; so buried in their feelings of fear are they. Misjudging spiritual intent, and anyone who abides spiritual intent, they do what they must to protect themselves, thus attempting to destroy others by word and deed. Destroying one by word is its own form of persecution and crucifixion. Neither need be physically implemented to affix their affect. Yet, if we pay no attention to such distractions, they have no power to affect us in any way. Once again, irony comes into play: these distractions turn back on the perpetrators as a negative form of karma.

'...they crucified him with two others, one on either side, Jesus being in the middle.'

As we take ourselves to the conscious mind, we find intellect paling in comparison to spiritual consciousness, and spiritual consciousness thus ascends as our primary—nay, our sole—realm of being. Our inherent divine will is freed into full expression, and we demonstrate Life only from this Source. God's will and ours come forth then as One, as divine will must, for there is not God—divine or spiritual consciousness—and something opposed to God. In this sense, it is we who have crucified ego consciousness—pushed it out of our awareness—so we may instead live true to our natural state, expressing divinity alone. And yet, even we cannot crucify something that does not exist. Still others, who have yet to come to this awareness, need not be judged, for to judge them is to make them separate from God and ourselves, which is not the Truth at all. Judge others not, then, for to judge another is to judge oneself. Bless all, as the perfect image and likeness of divine consciousness they are.

'His undergarment was seamless, woven in one piece from neck to hem.'

When we finally understand that we have but one way to live, out of spiritual consciousness, spiritual consciousness becomes a seamless garment we wear—and, with it, we both clothe and demonstrate our daily deliverance to the rest of the world. Those who would wish to separate us from this garment would wish to discard it altogether. After all, they would have no use for it themselves, except as some kind of token souvenir—which they could then easily cast away when they tired of it.

'After this, Jesus knew everything had been completed and, so that the scripture should be completely fulfilled...'

Giving up ego consciousness, we can finally declare Spirit to be what parents our way into the world. Endless streams of intuitional images, inspirations all, come to the fore, and we expel them forth as demonstration after demonstration of Truth discerned and practiced. Spiritual example is thus put out into the world. The last gasp of ego consciousness is put to rest and we thirst for Christ, spiritual consciousness—truly, as the One and only.

> 'This is the evidence of one who saw it—true evidence, and he knows that what he says is true—and he gives it so that you may believe as well.'

Giving oneself to spiritual consciousness neither needs nor casts outer signs, no proof in the material world at all. While it may seem that spiritual consciousness has been pierced and broken, those living in ego consciousness have no way of discerning such as reality. Though wishing to see outer signs of spiritual consciousness dying, the means for doing so—spiritual in nature—are seen only by those with eyes that really see: those inhabiting spiritual consciousness.

Shifting from ego consciousness, leaving it behind and moving to live only in the fullness of spiritual consciousness, our character also shifts to demonstrate only the Christ, spiritual consciousness. The dimension of spiritual consciousness and our character—as is so with our identity—become One. The old is laid to rest. Undeniably, even when feeling we have been crucified, we live beyond the feeling. This too passes. The body of consciousness we drop is entombed and we are clothed now in the sacred seamless garment, prepared now to live anew.

Chapter Twenty

'Till this moment they had not understood the scripture, that he must rise from the dead.'

As long as our new-found spiritual consciousness is seen as a bodily, human form, those who witness from this highly limited perspective will have missed the main message. The main message of ego consciousness, engaging ourselves in human love, based on healing separation by spiritualizing ego, hinders us in demonstrating the fullness of spiritual Love, Wisdom, Truth. Just as in material life, we cannot be in two places at once. Being in one prohibits us from being in another.

Should we be one who fluctuates between human love and spirituality, we cannot become firm in our commitment to the deeper realm of Spirit. We fluctuate between sensing Love as engagement with another human and feeling the much deeper feelings inhabiting and forming Soul. Soul Love is experienced as we connect deeply with All That Is in the Holy Relationship. Human love can point us inward, but is not inwardness itself. Confusion emanating out of ignorance or spiritual superficiality can be used as evidence that we, truly, have not arrived home— home to the validation of the Truth we are to abide and demonstrate. We feel lost, even abandoned—abandoned by what we took to be Truth. But now, at least we know we fell somewhat short in identifying with the deepest levels of Being.

'Do not cling to me, for I have not yet ascended...'

When we look to what has died in order to find Life, we bypass what Truth teaches us: to look only to Truth itself, where wholeness and Life and Wisdom not only live, but also flourish. To look at what has died in order to find Life would be like looking at the past or future in order to see the present. The present—Life—is found only here and now. Many are so busy coping with Life that they have yet to live Life, let alone savor Life. Rather than becoming despondent or depressed, we have the option of simply listening inward, paying attention to the Voice speaking in silence, so we may resonate with Truth instead of with feelings of separation and lack. When abiding sacred space—suddenly, like a visitation from angels—we hear Truth spoken. We comprehend that personal love cannot bind Wisdom and Truth; it cannot keep Wisdom and Truth from coming to fruition, represented by the fullness of Christ consciousness, the voice of authentic Love.

Closing the door to outsiders, those pernicious claims of ego consciousness, of duality, only heightens them in our mind. We give them power that they don't have when we try to protect ourselves from the claims. Claims to the contrary, we focus only on the Truth found in inner peace and poise, and Truth comes to us in all its splendor. Actually, Truth doesn't come to us at all. It is we who have allowed ourselves to become *aware* of Truth by putting ego conscious ways aside, parting the thin veil of unbelief, so we may clearly know Truth. The key to the door of Truth opens us to understand that when we look for spiritual Love where only human love is found, we will find it not. Neither can human love deter or hold back spiritual Love from fulfilling its charge.

When drawing our thoughts and images primarily from the unstable sea of ego consciousness, we mistakenly think we need outer signs in order to believe something is real. Reaching for outer signs is not a bad thing in itself; after all, doing so only points to our relationship to the human senses instead of inner resonance with Truth. This can be a sign used to our advantage. Each time we find ourselves looking for outer signs, instead of residing simply in inner Truth, we can use the signs to alert us of the need to change the direction of our walk a full 180 degrees:

from the journey of ego consciousness and outer signs, to The Inner Journey of spiritual awareness. The Inner Journey has only one imperative: that we listen inward, while deeper meaning seeks our awareness. This keeps the spiritual journey simple, indeed.

Sometimes we get caught up in our thoughts, those disciplines or archetypes that hold us in incompletion. Looking at Life through the lenses of any of the twelve archetypes highly limits our capability for seeing the whole, completeness. Strange as it may seem, completeness is all that exists, yet when looking through the glass darkly, we see completeness not. As we become clearer in comprehending that we are God and not any of the archetypes themselves, we go forth proclaiming by example the Truth regularly revealed to us in our completeness. We find and use these 'Keys to the Kingdom' as the unrelenting voice of Christ, spiritual consciousness. This eternal commitment to infinite Source is what forms the foundation of our spiritual Life. The celebration begins with trumpets blowing and angels singing, each a message of Love on the wings of a dove. We live each angelic message exactly this way.

Chapter Twenty-One: The Epilogue

'"Haven't you caught anything?...Throw the net out to starboard and you'll find something." So they threw the net out and could not haul it in because of the quantity of fish.'

Acting out of spiritual prompting and order, we find some of our compatriots still fishing for Truth in the sea of human senses. Needless to say—but I will, nevertheless—when fishing in a source of emotion for Truth, Truth cannot be caught. Again, when we look inward instead of outward for Truth, fishing on the other side of what usually carries us through Life—like a boat—the catch is so abundant, it is beyond harvesting all at once. Having followed our intuition into the seat of Wisdom, we are once again reinforced with spiritual validation and abundance. There is only one way to true abundance, to the treasures of the Kingdom, and it is by casting our nets inwardly, so inspiration may fill them to the brim, in unceasing numbers.

We feast on these gifts of the Kingdom endlessly, unfettered by human limitation. As we do feast, we see our newfound spiritual awareness opening us to the infinitude of spiritual nourishment, the one and only realm that orders our Life spiritually. Sometimes, it takes repeated reinforcement from within before we get the whole message. This is not to make us feel ashamed or feel guilty. This is just the way it works. So, if you feel you're almost Home—but not quite Home—you can be sure, Home is not far away. Often times, we need a full cycle of reminders, usually some component of three, to bring us Home. Such assurance is good enough to 'take to the bank', to serve as our spiritual currency.

Is there a price to pay for coming into spiritual reality? No, not really. Not when we understand that we are not given Truth for our use only. Truth is Light to shine on all, as the beacon lighting the spiritual path for others to also follow. Committing our lives to serve as beacons of Light is the highest and most profound source of Love. All else is nothing but a bad mistranslation, but a mere human emotion, a hollow facsimile of Truth.

Our journey, then, is both the means and the end, all rolled into One. We die to self so we may live Self to the ultimate. We lavish Love on all that is, *as* All That Is. Indeed, this is The Inward Journey we travel. And we and all we represent—the completeness of Love—live on, and on, and on...

A foolish consistency is the hobgoblin of little minds, adored by little statesmen and philosophers and divines. With consistency a great soul has simply nothing to do. He may as well concern himself with his shadow on the wall. Out upon your guarded lips! Sew them up with pockthread, do. Else if you would be a man speak what you think today in words as hard as cannon balls, and tomorrow speak what tomorrow thinks in hard words again, though it contradict everything you said today. Ah, then, exclaim the aged ladies, you shall be sure to be misunderstood! Misunderstood! It is a right fool's word. Is it so bad then to be misunderstood? Pythagoras was misunderstood, and Socrates and Jesus, and Luther, and Copernicus, and Galileo, and Newton, and every pure and wise spirit that ever took flesh.

Ralph Waldo Emerson
Self Reliant, an essay

About the Author

Dr. James H. (Jim) Young has served with distinction as a teacher and distinguished professor of higher education, and in a variety of leadership positions, including President of State University of New York at Potsdam and Chancellor of the University of Arkansas at Little Rock.

Jim is an award winning spiritual writer, poet and photographer who applies the reframing of spiritual perspective in all aspects of his life's calling. His photographs are regularly juried into national and international art and photography exhibitions and are found in collections around the world.

A ministerial graduate of the Pecos Benedictine Monastery's ecumenical school for spiritual directors and the Minister Emeritus of the Creative Life Church in Hot Springs, AR, Jim is also co-founder of the Arkansas Metaphysical Society in Eureka Springs, and The Aristotle Group in Hot Springs. The author of over a dozen spiritual books, Young is an inspirational teacher who takes participants to the threshold of their own Truth. Jim is available for workshops, presentations and seminars: www.creationspirit.net. To make arrangements, contact: 1andrea.thomas@gmail.com.

BOOKS

O is a symbol of the world, of oneness and unity. In different cultures it also means the "eye," symbolizing knowledge and insight. We aim to publish books that are accessible, constructive and that challenge accepted opinion, both that of academia and the "moral majority."

Our books are available in all good English language bookstores worldwide. If you don't see the book on the shelves ask the bookstore to order it for you, quoting the ISBN number and title. Alternatively you can order online (all major online retail sites carry our titles) or contact the distributor in the relevant country, listed on the copyright page.

See our website **www.o-books.net** for a full list of over 500 titles, growing by 100 a year.

And tune in to myspiritradio.com for our book review radio show, hosted by June-Elleni Laine, where you can listen to the authors discussing their books.

mySpiritRadio